Hands-On Python for DevOps

Leverage Python's native libraries to streamline your workflow
and save time with automation

Ankur Roy

Hands-On Python for DevOps

Group Product Manager: Preet Ahuja
Publishing Product Manager: Suwarna Rajput
Book Project Manager: Ashwin Kharwa
Senior Editor: Mohd Hammad
Technical Editor: Nithik Cheruvakodan
Copy Editor: Safis Editing
Proofreader: Safis Editing
Indexer: Pratik Shirodkar
Production Designer: Ponraj Dhandapani
DevRel Marketing Coordinator: Rohan Dobhal

First published: March 2024

Production reference: 1160224

Published by Packt Publishing Ltd.

Grosvenor House
11 St Paul's Square
Birmingham
B3 1RB, UK

ISBN 978-1-83508-116-7

www.packtpub.com

To my parents, who have always supported my choices and encouraged me to become a better person. To all my friends, peers, and colleagues, each of you has meant the world to me and I cannot begin to describe how you have shaped my life.

Contributors

About the author

Ankur Roy is a Solutions Architect at Online Partner AB in Stockholm, Sweden. Prior to this, he worked as a Software Engineer at Genese Solution in Kathmandu, Nepal. His areas of expertise include cloud-based solutions and workloads in a diverse range of fields such as development, DevOps, and security, among others. Ankur is an avid blogger, podcaster, content creator, and contributing member of the Python, DevOps, and cloud computing community. He has completed all the available certifications in Google Cloud and several others in AWS and Azure as well. Moreover, he is an AWS Community Builder.

I want to thank the entire Packt Publishing team for keeping me on track and focused on this book. I would also like to thank every person I told about writing this book for tolerating my exuberance for it.

About the reviewers

Shishir Subedi, an electronics and communications engineering graduate from the Institute of Engineering, Pulchowk Campus, discovered his passion for data science during his academic journey. Transitioning from a full stack Python developer to a part-time instructor at Ambikeshowri Campus, he focused on data mining and artificial intelligence, bridging theory and practice.

Currently a senior software engineer at Genese Solution, he leverages advanced language models to address financial technology challenges. Beyond his role, he contributes to education through training sessions for students and teachers, showcasing his commitment to technical proficiency and educational advancement.

Sagar Budhathoki, a dedicated Python/DevOps engineer, is recognized for his hands-on expertise in Python frameworks, system programming, and cloud computing. With a focus on automating and optimizing mission-critical deployments in AWS, Sagar leverages configuration management, CI/CD, and DevOps processes. His skills extend to Kubernetes deployment, OpenVPN configurations, and cybersecurity. As an AI/ML enthusiast, Sagar brings a comprehensive approach to technology, ensuring efficient, secure, and scalable solutions in the realm of DevOps.

Table of Contents

1

Introducing DevOps Principles   3

2

Talking about Python   19

3

The Simplest Ways to Start Using DevOps in Python Immediately   39

4

Provisioning Resources   53

Part 2: Sample Implementations of Python in DevOps

5

Manipulating Resources   67

6

Security and DevSecOps with Python   79

7

Automating Tasks   97

Part 3: Let's Go Further, Let's Build Bigger

10

11

MLOps and DataOps   153

12

How Python Integrates with IaC Concepts   165

13

The Tools to Take Your DevOps to the Next Level   177

Index   191

Other Books You May Enjoy   198

Preface

Welcome to this book! Let's talk about the content of this book and what you will learn from it. This book is about two things: DevOps and Python. It is about how these two entities, philosophies, frameworks, or whatever you would like to call them interact with each other.

This book will help you understand Python on a technical level, but also on a conceptual level, including what distinguishes Python from a lot of other languages and what makes it so popular among programmers and others who provide IT solutions.

At the same time, it will give you perspective on how important and useful DevOps is in modern IT infrastructure and how you can implement the concepts of DevOps using Python.

You will learn how to make the hard stuff easy and how to solve problems in a consistent and sustainable way. You will also learn how to insert bits of Python code into your workload to smoothen your problem-solving process.

This book will go beyond just some technical descriptions and processes and will help you make your workflow and work process even better regardless of the tools you are using.

Who this book is for

If you are even remotely concerned with DevOps or developing, you will find this book useful. But there are a few specific personas who may particularly find this book useful:

- **Developers looking to explore DevOps**: Since this is a book that uses a lot of code for DevOps, it is perfect for developers who may want to explore DevOps

- **DevOps engineers learning Python**: This book will help DevOps engineers who are learning Python and may want to try implementing some Python solutions in DevOps

- **People who like finding solutions**: If you're someone who wants to find solutions to IT problems and don't have a specific job title, but have a job to do, this book is for you

What this book covers

Chapter 1, *Introducing DevOps Principles*, will help you understand the concepts behind DevOps and how they are important in improving the productivity of your workload.

Chapter 2, *Talking about Python*, covers the core philosophical principles behind DevOps and how these principles define the approach that you take toward creating a solution.

Chapter 3, The Simplest Ways to Start Using DevOps in Python Immediately, provides a quick look at Python and the principles behind it, along with how these principles align with the principles of DevOps.

Chapter 4, Provisioning Resources, explores the easiest ways to use Python such that it could enhance your DevOps workload.

Chapter 5, Manipulating Resources, covers using Python as a means to provision resources in a sustainable and accurate way for your DevOps workload.

Chapter 6, Security and DevSecOps with Python, looks at modifying resources that already exist using Python in order to automate updates and mass modify replicated resources.

Chapter 7, Automating Tasks, explores using Python to automate common DevOps tasks and increase productivity for users by saving time on repetitive tasks.

Chapter 8, Understanding Event-Driven Architecture, covers using Python as a way to connect different systems to system architectures using event-driven concepts.

Chapter 9, Using Python for CI/CD Pipelines, looks at using Python for the most common DevOps task of Continuous Integration/Continuous Deployment (CI/CD) and enhancing these CI/CD pipelines.

Chapter 10, Common DevOps Use Cases in Some of the Biggest Companies in the World, looks at Python in DevOps use cases in the context of some of the biggest companies and workloads provided by the major cloud platforms.

Chapter 11, MLOps and DataOps, provides a look at the machine learning and big data niches of DevOps and how Python can help enhance these workloads.

Chapter 12, How Python Integrates with IaC Concepts, explores how Python libraries and frameworks are used to provision resources using infrastructure as code to build and modify DevOps workloads in a standardized way.

Chapter 13, The Tools to Take Your DevOps to the Next Level, looks at advanced DevOps concepts and tools and how they can be integrated into your workload.

To get the most out of this book

Often in this book, we cover tools and examples of how to use them to increase the productivity of your DevOps workload. You will need at least the version of Python mentioned here to use all the features described in the book. Most of the tasks done on one cloud platform can be done on equivalent services on other platforms.

Software/hardware covered in the book	Operating system requirements
Python 3.9 or higher	Windows, macOS, or Linux
Amazon Web Services (AWS)	
Google Cloud Platform (GCP)	
Microsoft Azure	
Google Colab	
Grafana	

For the cloud platforms, you will need to set up accounts and billing with the respective services.

If you are using the digital version of this book, we advise you to type the code yourself or access the code from the book's GitHub repository (a link is available in the next section). Doing so will help you avoid any potential errors related to the copying and pasting of code.

Download the example code files

You can download the example code files for this book from GitHub at https://github.com/ PacktPublishing/Hands-On-Python-for-DevOps. If there's an update to the code, it will be updated in the GitHub repository.

We also have other code bundles from our rich catalog of books and videos available at https:// github.com/PacktPublishing/. Check them out!

Conventions used

There are a number of text conventions used throughout this book.

`Code in text`: Indicates code words in text, database table names, folder names, filenames, file extensions, pathnames, dummy URLs, user input, and Twitter handles. Here is an example: "If you refer to the following diagram, the packet sizes are stored in the `packet_sizes` array and the timestamps of the packet are stored in the `timestamps` variable."

A block of code is set as follows:

```
def packet_handler(packet):
print(packet)
packet_sizes.append(len(packet))
timestamps.append(packet.time)
```

Any command-line input or output is written as follows:

```
pip install sphinx
```

Bold: Indicates a new term, an important word, or words that you see onscreen. For instance, words in menus or dialog boxes appear in **bold**. Here is an example: "With reference to the preceding figure, when you click the **Run** button shown at the top, you'll launch a Flask server (a URL that will return some sort of answer when it is called)."

> **Tips or important notes**
> Appear like this.

Get in touch

Feedback from our readers is always welcome.

General feedback: If you have questions about any aspect of this book, email us at customercare@ packtpub.com and mention the book title in the subject of your message.

Errata: Although we have taken every care to ensure the accuracy of our content, mistakes do happen. If you have found a mistake in this book, we would be grateful if you would report this to us. Please visit www.packtpub.com/support/errata and fill in the form.

Piracy: If you come across any illegal copies of our works in any form on the internet, we would be grateful if you would provide us with the location address or website name. Please contact us at copyright@packt.com with a link to the material.

If you are interested in becoming an author: If there is a topic that you have expertise in and you are interested in either writing or contributing to a book, please visit authors.packtpub.com.

Share Your Thoughts

Once you've read *Hands-On Python for DevOps*, we'd love to hear your thoughts! Scan the QR code below to go straight to the Amazon review page for this book and share your feedback.

https://packt.link/r/1835081169

Your review is important to us and the tech community and will help us make sure we're delivering excellent quality content.

Download a free PDF copy of this book

Thanks for purchasing this book!

Do you like to read on the go but are unable to carry your print books everywhere?

Is your eBook purchase not compatible with the device of your choice?

Don't worry, now with every Packt book you get a DRM-free PDF version of that book at no cost.

Read anywhere, any place, on any device. Search, copy, and paste code from your favorite technical books directly into your application.

The perks don't stop there, you can get exclusive access to discounts, newsletters, and great free content in your inbox daily

Follow these simple steps to get the benefits:

1. Scan the QR code or visit the link below

https://packt.link/free-ebook/9781835081167

2. Submit your proof of purchase

3. That's it! We'll send your free PDF and other benefits to your email directly

Part 1: Introduction to DevOps and role of Python in DevOps

This part will cover the basics of DevOps and Python and their relationship. It will also cover a few tricks and tips that could enhance your DevOps workload.

This part has the following chapters:

- *Chapter 1, Introducing DevOps Principles*
- *Chapter 2, Talking about Python*
- *Chapter 3, The Simplest Ways to Start Using DevOps in Python Immediately*
- *Chapter 4, Provisioning Resources*

Introducing DevOps Principles

Obey the principles without being bound by them.

– Bruce Lee

DevOps has numerous definitions, most of which are focused on culture and procedure. If you've gotten to the point where you have purchased this book as a part of your journey in the DevOps field, you have probably heard at least about 100 of these definitions. Since this is a book that focuses more on the hands-on, on-the-ground aspect of DevOps, we'll keep those abstractions and definitions to a minimum, or rather, explain them through actions rather than words whenever possible.

However, since this is a DevOps book, I am obliged to take a shot at this:

DevOps is a series of principles and practices that aims to set a culture that supports the automation of repetitive work and continuous delivery of a product while integrating the software development and IT operation aspects of product delivery.

Not bad. It's probably incomplete, but that's the nature of the beast, and that is perhaps what makes this definition somewhat appropriate. Any DevOps engineer would tell you that the work is never complete. Its principles are similar in many ways to the Japanese philosophy of **Ikigai**. It gives the engineers a purpose; an avenue for improvement on their systems which gives them the same thrill as a swordsman honing their skills or an artist painting their masterpiece. Satisfied, yet unsatisfied at the same time. Zen.

Philosophical musings aside, I believe DevOps principles are critical to any modern software team. To work on such teams, it is better to start with the principles as they help explain a lot of how the tools used in DevOps were shaped, how and why software teams are constructed the way they are, and to facilitate DevOps principles. If I had to sum it up in one word: time.

In this chapter, you will learn about the basic principles that define DevOps as a philosophy and a mindset. It is important to think of this just as much as an exercise in ideology as it is in technology. This chapter will give you the context you need to understand why DevOps principles and tools exist and the underlying philosophies behind them.

In this chapter, we will cover the following topics:

- Exploring automation
- Understanding logging and monitoring
- Incident and event response
- Understanding high availability
- Delving into infrastructure as a code

Exploring automation

We're going to start with why **automation** is needed in life in general and then we'll move toward a more specific definition that relates to DevOps and other tech team activities. Automation is for the lazy, but many do not realize how hard you must work and how much you must study to truly be lazy. To achieve automation, it requires a mindset, an attitude, a frustration with present circumstances.

Automation and how it relates to the world

In Tim Ferris's book *The 4-Hour Workweek*, he has an entire section dedicated to automating the workflow which emphasizes the fact that the principle of automation helps you clean up your life and remove or automate any unnecessary tasks or distractions. DevOps hopes to do something similar but in your professional life. Automation is the primary basis that frees up our time to do other things we want.

One of the things mankind has always tried to automate even further is transportation. We have evolved from walking to horses to cars to planes to self-driving versions of those things. The reason for that is the same reason DevOps became a prominent culture: to save time.

How automation evolves from the perspective of an operations engineer

You may have heard the famous story of the build engineer who automated his entire job down to the second (if you haven't looked it up, it's a great read). What he did was he automated any task within the server environment that required his attention for more than 90 seconds (solid DevOps principles from this guy if you ask me). This included automatically texting his wife if he was late, automated rollback of database servers based on a specific e-mail sent by a client's database administrator, and Secure Shelling into the coffee machine to automatically serve him coffee, further proving my point that most things can be automated.

You don't need to automate your workspace or your life to this extent if you don't want to, but here's the lesson you should take away from this: use automation to save time and prevent yourself from being hassled, because a) your time is precious and b) an automated task does the job perfectly every time if you set it correctly just once.

Let's take ourselves through the life of a young software engineer named John. Let's say John is a Flask developer. John has just joined his first big-boy software team and they are producing something already in production with a development and testing environment. John has only worked on `localhost:5000` his entire programming journey and knows nothing past that (a lot of entry-level coders don't). John knows you use Git for version control and that the source code you push up there goes... somewhere. Then it shows up in the application. Here's John's journey figuring it out (and then being bored by it):

- John gets access to the repository and sets up the code locally. While it's nothing he's never done before, he starts contributing code.

- A month later, an Operations guy who was managing the deployment of the specific service John was working on leaves. John is asked if he can take over the deployments while they hire a replacement. John, being young and naïve, agrees.

- Two months later, with no replacement yet, John has figured out how deployment servers such as Nginx or Apache work and how to copy his code onto a server environment and deploy it in a way that it can reach the public internet (it turns out it was essentially just `localhost` in disguise. Who knew?). He may have even been allowed to modify the DNS records all by himself.

- Four months later, John is tired, he spends half his time pulling code into the server, solving merge conflicts, restarting the server, and debugging the server. The server is a herd of goats, and he is but one hand with many mouths to feed. It becomes difficult for him to push new features and finish his pre-assigned tasks. This is when he starts wondering if there is a better way.

- He learns about bash scripting and runbooks. He learns that you can add triggers to both the repository and the server to perform certain tasks when the code has been updated. He also learns about playbooks that can be run when a common error starts popping up.

- Six months later, John has automated practically every part of the deployment and maintenance procedures for the application. It runs itself. The process has made John a better coder as well as he now writes his code with the challenges of deployment and automation in mind.

- Eight months later, John has nothing to do. He's automated all relevant tasks, and he doesn't need that Ops guy that HR never got back to him about. He is now a DevOps engineer.

- His manager asks him why his worklog seems empty. John tells him that DevOps tasks are measured by difficulty and complexity and not work hours. The manager is confused.

- Now, at this point, one of two things happens: either the manager listens and John pushes his enterprise toward a DevOps philosophy that will transform it into a modern IT company (there are antiquated IT companies, weird as that may seem), or he leaves for a place that appreciates his talents, which would be pretty easy to do if he markets them correctly.

This may seem like a fantasy, but it's how many DevOps engineers are forged: in the fires of incompetence. This tale is, however, meant to be more analogous to companies as a whole and whether they transform to use DevOps principles or not. The ones that do become more agile and capable of delivering new features and using resources toward something as opposed to using them just to maintain something.

Automation is born out of a desire to not do the same things differently (usually for the worse) over and over again. This concept is at the heart of DevOps, since the people who automate realize how important it is to have consistency in repetitive tasks and why it is a time and potentially a lifesaver.

But for a task to be reliably done in the same way over and over again, it must be observed so that it can be kept on the correct path. That is where logging and monitoring come in.

Understanding logging and monitoring

Switching to a more grounded topic, one of the driving principles of DevOps is logging and monitoring instances, endpoints, services, and whatever else you can track and trace. This is necessary because regardless of whatever you do, how clean your code is, or how good your server configuration is, something will fail, go wrong, or just inexplicably stop working altogether. This will happen. It's a fact of life. It is in fact, Murphy's law:

> *Anything that can go wrong will go wrong at the worst possible time.*

Familiarizing yourself with this truth is important for a DevOps engineer. Once you have acknowledged it, then you can deal with it. Logging and monitoring come in because when something *does* go wrong, you need the appropriate data to respond to that event, sometimes automatically.

The rest of this section has been laid out in terms of logging, monitoring, and alerts. Each one of these aspects plays an important role in keeping the DevOps train (workload) on the right track.

Logging

If you are not from a technical background or are new to logging principles, think of logging in this way:

Every day after school, a schoolboy would go to an old woman selling matches and give her money for one matchbox. However, he'd take no matchboxes in return. Then one day, as the boy went about his usual routine, he saw the woman about to speak up and he said, "I know you're probably wondering why I give you money for the matchbox but don't take one in return. Would you like me to tell you?" The woman replied, "No, I just wanted to tell you that the price of matches has gone up."

In this case, the woman is the logger, and the boy is the person viewing the log. The woman doesn't care about the reason. She's just collecting the data, and when the data changes, she collects the changed data. The boy checks in every day and goes about his routine uninterrupted until something changes in the log. Once the log changes, the boy decides whether to react or not depending on what he would consider to be an appropriate response.

In subsequent chapters, you'll learn about logs, how to analyze them (usually with Python), and appropriate responses to logs. But at present, all you need to know is that good bookkeeping/logging has built empires because history and the lessons that we learn from it are important. They give us perspective and the appropriate lessons that we need to respond to future events.

Monitoring

When you look at the title of this section, *Understanding logging and monitoring*, some of you might wonder, what's the difference? Well, that's valid. It took me a while to figure that out as well. And I believe that it comes down to a couple of things:

1. **Monitoring** looks at a specific metric (usually generated by logs) and whether or not that metric has passed a certain threshold. However, **logging** is simply collecting the data without generating any insight or information from it.

2. Monitoring is active and focuses on the current state of an instance or object that is being monitored, whereas logging is passive and focuses more on the collection of largely historical data.

In many ways, it is like the differences between a transactional database and a data warehouse. One functions on current data while the other is about storing historical data to find trends. Both are intertwined with each other nearly inexorably and thus are usually spoken of together. Now that you have logged and monitored all the data, you might ask yourself, what is it for? The next section will help with that.

Alerts

You cannot have a conversation about logging and monitoring without bringing up the concept of alerts. A **logged metric** is monitored by a monitoring service. This service looks at the data produced from the logs and measures it against a threshold that is set for that metric. If the threshold is crossed for a sustained, defined period of time, an **alert** or alarm is raised.

Most of the time, these alerts or alarms are either connected to a notification system that can inform the necessary personnel regarding the heightened alarm state, or a response system that can automatically trigger a response to the event.

Now that you have learned about the powers of observation and insight that you gain from logging and monitoring, it is time to learn how to wield that power. Let's find out the actions we should take when we find significant and concerning insights through logging and monitoring.

Incident and event response

I'm going to put Murphy's Law here again because I cannot state this enough:

> *Anything that can go wrong will go wrong at the worst possible time.*

Dealing with **incident and event response** involves either a lot of work or zero work. It depends on how prepared you are and how unique the incident or event is. Incident and event response covers a lot of ground from automation and cost control, to cybersecurity.

How a DevOps engineer responds to an event depends on a great number of things. In terms of dealing with clients and customers, a **Service Level Objective** (**SLO**) is used when a response is necessary. However, this is largely on production environments and requires the definition of a **Service Level Indicator** (**SLI**). It also involves the creation of an error budget to determine the right time to add new features and what the right time is to work on the maintenance of a system. Lower-priority development environments are used to stress test potential production cases and the effectiveness of incident response strategies. These objectives will be further explored in the *Understanding high availability* section.

If you work on the **Site Reliability Engineering** (**SRE**) side of DevOps, then incidents are going to be your bread and butter. A large part of the job description for that role involves having the correct metrics set up so that you can respond to a situation. Many SRE teams are set up these days to have active personnel around the globe who can monitor sites according to their active time zones. The response to the incident itself is done by an **incident response team** which I will cover in detail in the next section.

Another part of incident response is the understanding of what caused the incident, how long it took to recover, and what could have been done better in the future. This is covered by **post-mortems**, which usually assist in the creation of a clear, unbiased report that can help with future incidents. The incident response team is responsible for the creation of this document.

How to respond to an incident (in life and DevOps)

Incidents happen, and the people who are responsible for dealing with these incidents need to handle them. Firefighters have to battle fires, doctors have to treat the sick, and DevOps engineers have to contend with a number of incidents that can occur when running the sites that they manage and deploy.

Now, in life, how would you deal with an incident or something that affects your life or your work that you need to deal with? There's one approach that I read in a book called *Mental Strength* by Iain Stuart Abernathy that I subsequently found everywhere among the DevOps courses and experts that I met: **Specific, Measurable, Achievable, Realistic, and Time-bound** (**SMART**). If a solution to a problem has to follow all of these principles, it will have a good chance of working. You can apply this to your own life along with your DevOps journey. It's all problem-solving, after all.

To define the SMART principle in brief, let's go over each of the components one by one:

- Specific: Know exactly what is happening
- Measurable: Measure its impact
- Achievable: Think of what your goal is for mitigation

- Realistic: Be realistic with your expectations and what you can do
- Time-bound: Time is of the essence, so don't waste it

Here are some common incidents DevOps engineers may have to deal with:

- The production website or application goes down
- There is a mass spike in traffic suggesting a distributed denial-of-service attack
- There is a mass spike in traffic suggesting an influx of new users that will require an upscale in resources
- There is an error in building the latest code in the code pipeline
- Someone deleted the production database (seriously, this can happen)

Dealing with incidents involves first dividing the incident based on the type of response that can be provided and whether this type of incident has been anticipated and prepared for. If the response is manual, then time isn't a factor. Usually, this occurs if an incident doesn't affect the workload but must be addressed, such as a potential anomaly or a data breach. The stakeholders need to be told so that they can make an informed decision on the matter. Automatic responses are for common errors or incidents that you know occur from time to time and have the appropriate response for. For example, if you need to add more computing power or more servers in response to increased traffic or if you have to restart an instance if a certain metric goes awry (this happens quite a bit with Kubernetes).

We deal with these incidents in order to provide the maximum availability possible for any application or site that we manage. This practice of aiming for maximum availability will be covered in the next section on site reliability engineering.

Site reliability engineering

So, **site reliability engineering** (**SRE**) is considered a form of DevOps by many and is considered to be separate from DevOps by others. I'm putting this section in here because, regardless of your opinion on the subject, you as a DevOps Engineer will have to deal with the concepts of site reliability, how to maintain it, and how to retain customer trust.

SRE as a concept is more rigid and inflexible than the DevOps philosophy as a whole. It is the evolution of the data center technicians of the past who practically lived in data centers for the course of their careers, maintaining server racks and configurations to ensure whatever product that was being delivered by their servers would continue to be delivered. That was their job: not creating anything new, but finding solutions to maintain their old infrastructure.

SRE is similar, but the engineer has been taken out of the data center and placed inside a remote work desk at an office or their own home. They still live fairly close to their data center or the cloud region containing the resources that they manage, but they differ from their predecessors in a couple of ways:

1. Their teams are likely scattered across their regions as opposed to being in a singular place.

2. Their emphasis is now on what we call *predictive maintenance*, i.e. they do not wait for something to go wrong to respond.

Incident response teams

This new trend of SRE also helped produce incident response teams, which can be quickly created from within the ranks of the DevOps team to monitor and deal with an incident. They can do so while communicating with stakeholders to keep them informed about the situation and finding the root cause of the incident. These teams also produce reports that can help the DevOps team deal with and mitigate such potential situations in the future. In a world where an outage of a few minutes can sometimes cause millions of dollars of loss and damage, incident response teams have become a prominent part of any DevOps engineer's world.

Usually, an incident response team is made up of the following members:

- **Incident commander (IC)**: An incident commander leads the response to the incident and is responsible for a post-incident response plan

- **Communications leader (CL)**: A communications leader is the public-facing member of the team who is responsible for communicating the incident and the progress made to mitigate the incident to the stakeholders

- **Operations leader (OL)**: Sometimes synonymous with the incident commander, the OL leads the technical resolution of the incident by looking at logs, errors, and metrics and figures out a way to bring the site or application back online

- **Team members**: Team members under the CL and OL who are coordinated by their respective leaders for whatever purpose they may require

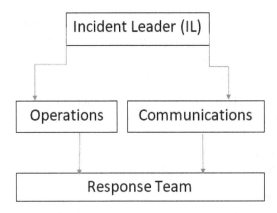

Figure 1.1 – A typical incident response team structure

As you can see in *Figure 1.1*, the structure of the incident response team is fairly simple and is usually quite effective in mitigating an incident when such a case arises. But what happens after the incident? Another incident? That's a possibility and the fact that it's a possibility is the exact reason we need to gain insight from the current incident. We do this with post-mortems.

Post-mortems

An incident happens. It affects business value and the users of the application, and then it goes away or is solved. But what's to say it doesn't happen again? What could be done to mitigate it before it even has the chance to happen again? Post-mortems are the answer to all of that. Any good DevOps team will perform a post-mortem after an incident has occurred. This post-mortem will be led by the incident response team that handled the situation.

Post-mortems sound macabre, but they are an essential part of the healing process and improvement of a workload and a DevOps team. They let the DevOps team understand the incident that occurred and how it happened, and they dissect the response made by the response team. Exercises such as these create a solid foundation for faster response times in the future as well as for learning experiences and team growth.

One of the aspects of post-mortems that is constantly emphasized is that they must be blameless, i.e., there mustn't be any placing of responsibility for the cause of the incident upon an individual. If an incident has occurred, it is the process that must be modified, not the person. This approach creates an environment of openness and makes sure that the results of the post-mortem are factual, objective, and unbiased.

So, you may ask yourself, why go through all of this? The reason is often contractual and obligatory. In a modern technological landscape, things such as these are necessary and expected to deliver value and availability to the end user. So let's understand exactly what that availability means.

Understanding high availability

I'm not going to state Murphy's Law a third time, but understand that it applies here as well. Things will go wrong and they will fall apart. Never forget that. One of the reasons DevOps as a concept and culture became so popular was that its techniques delivered a highly available product with very little downtime, maintenance time, and vulnerability to app-breaking errors.

One of the reasons DevOps succeeds in its mission for high availability is the ability to understand failure, react to failure, and recover from failure. Here's a famous quote from Werner Vogel, the CTO of Amazon:

Everything fails, all the time.

This is, in fact, the foundation of the best practice guides, tutorials, and documentation that AWS makes for DevOps operations, and it's true. Sometimes, things fail because of a mistake that has been made. Sometimes, they fail because of circumstances that are completely out of our control, and sometimes, things fail for no reason. But the point is that things fail, and when they do, DevOps engineers need to deal with those failures. Additionally, they need to figure out how to deal with them as fast as possible with as little disturbance to the customer as possible.

A little advice for people who may have never worked on a solid project before, or at least been the guy facing the guy giving orders: *ask for specifics*. It's one of the tenets of DevOps, Agile, and any other functional strategy and is vital to any sort of working relationship between all the stakeholders and participants of a project. If you tell people exactly what you want, and if you give them metrics that define that thing, it becomes easier to produce it. So, in DevOps, there are metrics and measurements that help define the requirements for the availability of services as well as agreements to maintain those services.

There are a number of acronyms, metrics, and indicators that are associated with high availability. These are going to be explored in this section and they will help define exactly what high availability means in a workload.

SLIs, SLOs, and SLAs

Agreements of service, terms of services, contracts, and many other types of agreements are designed so that two parties in agreement with one another can draw out that agreement and are then beholden to it. You need a contract when one party pays another for a service, when two parties exchange services, when one party agrees to a user agreement drawn up by the other party (ever read one of those?), and for a lot of other reasons.

Let's break down what each of these are:

- **Service level indicators** (**SLIs**): These are metrics that can be used to numerically define the level of service that is being provided by a product. For instance, if you were to run a website, you could use the uptime (the amount of time the website is available for service) as an SLI.

- **Service level objectives** (**SLOs**): These provide a specific number to the aforementioned SLIs. That number is an objective that the DevOps team must meet for their client. Going back to the previous example in the SLI definition: if uptime is the SLI, then having an uptime of 99% a month is the SLO. Typically, a month has 30 days, which is 720 hours, so the website should have a minimum uptime of 712.8 hours in that month with a tolerable downtime of 7.2 hours.

- **Service level agreements** (**SLAs**): These are contracts that enforce an SLO. In an SLA, there is a defined SLO (hope you're keeping up now) for an SLI which must be achieved by the DevOps team. If this SLA is not fulfilled, the party that contracted the DevOps team is entitled to some compensation. Concluding that example, if there is an SLA for that website with an SLO of 99% uptime, then that is defined in the agreement and that is the metric that needs to be fulfilled by the DevOps team. However, most SLAs have more than one SLO.

To put it simply, SLIs (are measured for) -> SLOs (are defined in) -> SLAs.

One of the more prominent examples of an SLA that the AWS team likes to show off is the 11 9s (99.999999999%) of durability for Amazon's **Secure Storage Service (S3)** (other cloud object storage services do the same as well). This means that any S3 bucket loses one object every 10,000 years. It also has a 99.9% availability for its standard-tier SLA. This is equivalent to being down for 44 minutes out of a calendar month of 30 days.

Now, these three abbreviations are related to availability, but in an ancillary way. The next two abbreviations will be much more focused on what availability actually entails contractually and goal-wise.

RTOs and RPOs

These two abbreviations are much more availability-focused than the other three. **Recovery Time Objectives (RTOs)** and **Recovery Point Objectives (RPOs)** are used as measuring sticks to measure the borders of availability. If an application fails to fall within its RTO or RPO then it hasn't fulfilled its guarantee of availability. RTOs and RPOs are largely concerned with recovering operations after a disaster. There are financial, medical, and other critical systems in this world that wouldn't be able to function if their underlying systems went down for even a few minutes. And given the *everything fails all the time* motto, that disaster or failure is not unrealistic.

An RTO is placed on a service when there is a need for a service to constantly be up and the time used in RTO is the amount of time that a service can afford to be offline before it recovers and comes online again. The fulfillment of an RTO is defined in the SLA as the maximum time that a system will be down before it is available again. To be compliant with the SLA that the DevOps has, they must recover the system within that time frame.

Now, you may think this is easy: just turn the thing on and off again, right? Well, in many cases that'll do the job, but remember that this is not about just doing the job, it's about doing the job within a set amount of time.

In most cases, when a server goes down, restarting the server will do the trick. But how long does that trick take? If your RTO is five minutes and you take six minutes to restart your server, you have violated your RTO (and in a lot of critical enterprise systems, the RTO is lower than that). This is why, whenever you define RTOs initially, you should do two things: propose for more time than you have and think with automation.

Modern SLAs of 99% (seven hours a month) or even 99.9% (44 minutes a month) are achieved through the removal of human interaction (specifically, hesitation) from the process of recovery. Services automatically recover through constant monitoring of their health so when an instance shows signs of unhealthiness, it can either be corrected or replaced. This concept is what gave rise to the popularity of Kubernetes which in its production form has the best recovery and health check concepts on the market.

RPOs are different in that they are largely related to data and define a specific date or time (point) which the data in a database or instance can be restored from. The RPO is the maximum tolerable difference of time between the present and the date of the backup or recovery point. For example, a database of users on a smaller internal application can have an RPO of one day. But a business-critical application may have an RPO of only a few minutes (if that).

RPOs are maintained through constant backups and replicas of databases. The database in most applications that you use isn't the primary database but a **read replica** that is often placed in a different geographical region. This alleviates the load from the primary database, leaving it open for exclusive use for writing operations. If the database does go down, it can usually be recovered very quickly by promoting one of the read replicas into the new primary. The read will have all of the necessary data, so consistency is usually not a problem. In the event of a disaster in a data center, such backup and recovery options become very important for restoring system functions.

Based on these objectives and agreements, we can come up with metrics that can affect team behavior, like our next topic.

Error budgets

In a team following DevOps principles, error budgets become a very important part of the direction that the team takes in the future. An error budget is calculated with this formula: *Error budget = 1-SLA (in decimal)*

What this basically means is that *an error budget is the percentage left over from the SLA*. So, if there is an SLA of 99%, then the error budget would be 1%. It is the downtime to our uptime. In this case, the error budget per month would be around 7.2 hours. According to this budget, we can define how our team can progress based on team goals:

- If the team's goal is reliability, then the objective should be to tighten the error budget. Doing this will help the team deliver a higher SLO and gain more trust from their customers. If you tighten an SLO from 99% to 99.9%, you are reducing the tolerable downtime from 7.2 hours to 44 minutes, so you need to ensure that you can deliver on such a promise. Inversely, if you cannot deliver on such an SLO, then you shouldn't promise it in any sort of agreement.

- If the team's goal is developing new features, then it mustn't come at the cost of a decreased SLO. If a large amount of the error budget is being consumed every month, then the team should pivot from working on new features to making the system more reliable.

All these statistics exist to help us have metrics that can be used to maintain high availability. But we aren't the ones who will use them, we will simply configure them to be used automatically.

How to automate for high availability?

Now that you know the rules of the game, you need to figure out how to work within the rules and deliver on the promises that you have given your customers. To accomplish this, you simply have to accomplish the things that have been set in your SLAs. Not particularly difficult on a small scale, but we're not here to think small.

There are some essentials that every DevOps engineer needs to know to accomplish high availability:

- Using desired state configurations on virtual machines to prevent state drift
- How to properly backup data and recover it quickly in the event of a disaster
- How to automate recovery of servers and instances with minimal downtime
- How to properly monitor workloads for signs of errors or disruptions
- How to succeed, even when you fail

Sounds easy, doesn't it? Well, in a way it is. All these things are interconnected and woven into the fabric of DevOps and depend upon each other. To recover success from failure is one of the most important skills to learn in life, not just in DevOps.

This concept of failure and recovering back to a successful state has been taken even further by the DevOps community through the development of tools that maintain the necessary state of the workload through code.

Delving into infrastructure as a code

Finally, in a book about Python, we get to a section about code. So far, I've given you a lot of information about what needs to be accomplished but to accomplish the things we want especially in this book, we must have a method, a tool, a weapon, i.e., code.

Now the word "code" scares a lot of people in the tech industry, even developers. It's weird being afraid of the thing that is under everything you work with. But that's the reality sometimes. If you, dear reader, are such a person, first off, it's a brave thing to purchase this book, and secondly, all you are doing is denying yourself the opportunity to solve all the problems you have in the world. Seriously.

Now, the reason is that code is the weapon of choice in almost every situation. It is the solution to all your automation problems, monitoring problems, response problems, contract problems, and maybe other problems that you may have that I don't know about. And a lot of it requires a minimal amount of code.

> **Important note**
> Remember this: the amateur writes no code, the novice writes a lot of code and the expert writes code in a way that it seems like they've written nothing at all, so expect a lot of code in this book.

Let me explain further. To maintain the consistency of service required by DevOps, you need something constant; something that your resources can fall back on that they can use to maintain themselves to a standard. You can write code for that.

In addition to that, you need to be able to automate repetitive tasks and tasks that require reactions faster than what a human being can provide. You need to free up your own time while also not wasting your client's time. You can write code for that.

You also need to be flexible and capable of dynamically creating resources regardless of the change in environment as well as the ability to switch over to backups, failovers, and alternates seamlessly. You can write code for that.

Infrastructure as code (**IaC**) is particularly useful for that last part. In fact, you can use it to encapsulate and formulate the other two as well. IaC is the orchestrator. It gives the cloud services a proverbial *shopping list* of things it wants and the configuration it wants them in and in exchange for that, and it gets the exact configuration that was coded on it.

The fact that IaC is a *get-exactly-what-you-want* system is a word of caution because as with everything involving computers, it will do *exactly* what you want, which means you need to be very specific and precise when using these frameworks.

Let's look at a little sample that we will use to demonstrate the concept behind IaC using some simple pseudocode (without any of that pesky syntax).

Pseudocode

I'm not going to write any actual code for IaC in this chapter (you can find that in the chapter dedicated to IaC), I'm just going to give a quick overview of the concept behind IaC using some pseudocode definitions. These will help you understand how singular IaC definitions work in securing resources.

An example pseudocode – to create a virtual machine - broken down into the simplest pieces would be something like the following:

- `Module Name` (Usually descriptive of the service being deployed)

  - `VM Name` (say VM1)

  - `Resources allocated` (Specifications, or class of VM) (say 1 GB RAM)

  - Internal networking and IP addresses (in `VPC1`)

  - Tags (say `"Department": "Accounting"`)

This example will create a VM named VM1, with 1 GB of RAM in a VPC or equivalent network named VPC1 with a tag of key `Department` with an `Accounting` value. Once launched, that is exactly what will happen. Oops, I needed 2 GB of RAM. What do I do now?

That's easy, just change your code:

- `Module Name` (Usually descriptive of the service being deployed)

  - `VM Name` (say `VM1`)
  - `Resources allocated` (Specifications, or class of VM) (now its 2GB RAM)
  - Internal networking and IP addresses (in `VPC1`)
  - Tags (say `"Department": "Accounting"`)

And that's how easy that is. You can see why it's popular. It is stable enough to be reliable, but flexible enough to be reusable. Now, here are a couple of other pointers that will help you understand how most IaC templates work:

- If you had renamed the VM, it would have been redeployed with the new name
- If you had renamed the module, most templates would by default tear down and decommission the old VM in the old module and create a new one from scratch
- Changing the network or VPC would logically move the VM to the other network whose network rules it would now follow
- Most templates would allow you to loop or iterate over multiple VMs

IaC, man what a concept. It's a very interesting – and very popular – solution to a common problem. It can solve a lot of DevOps headaches and should be in the arsenal of every DevOps engineer.

Summary

The concept of DevOps is exciting, vast, and has room to get creative. It is a discipline where the world is essentially at your command. Effective DevOps requires effective structure and adaptation of that structure to a challenge as we learned in our *Exploring automation* section.

But remember, *anything that can go wrong will go wrong*, so plan for success but prepare for the fact that failure is a common occurrence. In such cases of failure – as we learned in the sections about monitoring and event response – the ability to recover is what matters, and the speed of that recovery also matters quite often. If an incident to be recovered from is new, it must be reported and understood so that such incidents can be mitigated in the future.

And lastly, as we covered in *Delving into infrastructure as a code*, code is your friend. Be nice to your friends and play with them. You'll learn how to in this book.

2

Talking about Python

Language is the key to world peace. If we all spoke each other's tongues, perhaps the scourge of war would be ended forever.

– Batman

The Python programming language was built on a set of principles that was meant to simplify coding in it. This simplification came at the cost of a lot of speed and performance compared to other programming languages but also produced a popular language that was accessible and easy to build in, with a massive library of built-in functions. All of these made Python very versatile and capable of being used in a myriad of situations, a programming Swiss army knife if you will. A perfect tool for a diverse discipline such as **DevOps**.

Beginners are recommended Python as a learning language because it is fairly simple, easy to pick up, and also used a fair amount in the industry (if it wasn't, why would I be writing this book?). Python is also a great flexible programming language for hobbyists because of the same reasons as before, as well as the library support that it has for things such as OS automation, the internet of things, machine learning, and other specific areas of interest. At the professional level, Python has a lot of competition for market space, but this is largely because – at that level – smaller differences, legacy systems, and available skills count for something.

And that's perfectly fine. We don't need the entire market share for Python – that would be very boring and counterintuitive to innovation. In fact, I encourage you to try other languages and their concepts before returning to Python because that will help you find out a lot of things that Python makes easier for you and help you appreciate the abstraction that Python provides.

Python is the language of simplicity, and it is the language of conciseness. Often, you can write a piece of code in Python in one line that would have otherwise taken 10 lines in another language.

All the things that I have stated are not the only reasons that Python is so popular in development and DevOps. In fact, one of the most important reasons for Python's popularity is this:

Yes, that. That is not a print error. That represents the JSON/dictionary format that carries data across the internet on practically every major modern system. Python handles that better than any other language and makes it easier to operate on than any other language. The base Python libraries are usually enough to fully unleash the power of JSON whereas in many other languages, it would require additional libraries or custom functions.

Now, you might ask, "Can't I install those libraries? What's the big deal?" Well, understanding the big deal comes from working with this type of data and understanding that not every programming language that you use has grown to emphasize the importance of these two brackets and how much of a problem that can become in modern DevOps/the cloud.

In this chapter, I will provide a basic refresher for Python and give you some Python knowledge that is practical, hands-on, and useful in the DevOps field. It will not be all of the Python programming language, because that is a massive topic and not the focus of this book. We will only focus on the aspects of the Python programming language that are useful for our work.

So, let's list out what we are going to cover here:

- The basics of Python through the philosophical ideas of its creators
- How Python can support DevOps practices
- Some examples to support these points

Python 101

Python is – as I have said before – a simple language to pick up. It is meant to be readable by the layperson and the logic of its code is meant to be easily understandable. It is because of this fact that everything from installing Python to configuring it in your OS is probably the smoothest installation process out of any of the major programming languages. The barrier of entry is next to zero.

So, if you want to declare a variable and other basic stuff, start from the following figure and figure it out:

```
a=12
print(a, type(a))
12 <class 'int'>
b="if you cant figure this out what're you doing here"
print(b, b.upper())
if you cant figure this out what're you doing here IF YOU CANT FIGURE THIS OUT WHAT'RE YOU DOING HERE
```

Figure 2.1 – Declaring and manipulating variables

This section will be focused on the philosophy of Python because that is what will be important in your journey toward using Python in DevOps. Once you understand the underlying philosophies, you will understand why Python and DevOps are such a perfect match.

In fact, we can find that similarity in the **Zen of Python**. The Zen is a series of principles that have come to define the Python language and how its libraries are built. The Zen of Python was written in 1999 by Tim Peters for his Python mailing list. It has since been integrated into the Python interpreter itself. If you go to the command line of the interpreter and type in `import this`, you'll see the 19 lines of Zen. Odd number, you say? It's an interesting story.

So, if you haven't seen it before, I'm going to list it out here for posterity:

Beautiful is better than ugly.

Explicit is better than implicit.

Simple is better than complex.

Complex is better than complicated.

Flat is better than nested.

Sparse is better than dense.

Readability counts.

Special cases aren't special enough to break the rules.

Although practicality beats purity.

Errors should never pass silently.

Unless explicitly silenced.

In the face of ambiguity, refuse the temptation to guess.

There should be one-- and preferably only one --obvious way to do it.

Although that way may not be obvious at first unless you're Dutch.

Now is better than never.

Although never is often better than *right* now.

If the implementation is hard to explain, it's a bad idea.

If the implementation is easy to explain, it may be a good idea.

Namespaces are one honking great idea -- let's do more of those!

(*Tim Peters, 1999, The Zen of Python,* `https://peps.python.org/pep-0020/#the-zen-of-python`)

The reason I'm laying this out for you right now is so that I can give you examples of how these principles have become a part of the fully evolved Python language. I am going to do this in pairs. Except for that last one. These rules and their implementations will provide you with the appropriate boundaries that you need to write decent Python code.

Beautiful-ugly/explicit-implicit

Let's start with beauty. They say beauty is in the eye of the beholder. And this is why, when you behold improperly indented code, you begin to understand the beauty of actually indented code. Here is the same code written correctly in JavaScript and Python:

- JavaScript:

```
const value = 5; for (let i = 0; i <= value; i++) {console.
log(i);}
```

- Python:

```
value = 5
for i in range(value+1):
print(i)
```

The JavaScript code works, by the way. It does the same thing that the Python code does. You could write all of the scripts for JavaScript on a single line if you wanted to (and when you build JS frontends, sometimes you do to save space). But which one can you read better? Which one breaks down the information in a better way for you? Python forces this syntax due to its removal of semi-colons in favor of indentations as a way to separate code lines, making the code more objectively *beautiful*.

But something is missing. You may understand the fact that the code is clear and concise, but you might not understand the code. This is where we must be explicit, in the definition of the code and its variables. Python encourages comments describing every code block as well as a defined structure when it comes to assigning variables. **Snake case** (`snake_case`) is used for variables and uppercase snake case is used for constants. Let's re-write our Python code following these guidelines:

```
""" Initial constant that doesn't change """
INITIAL_VALUE = 5
""" Loop through the range of the constant """
for current_value in range(INITIAL_VALUE+1):
""" Print current loop value """
print(current_value)
```

You don't need to do this for every line; I'm just being a little more explicit than usual for posterity. But this is the basic way to define variables and comments. No more of that *i*, *j*, and *k* stuff. Be kind and be defined.

Definition simplifies things, which is what we are going to discuss in this next section.

Simple-complex-complicated

Simplicity must be maintained wherever possible. That is the rule because, well, it's easier that way. Keeping things simple, however, is hard. It's impossible sometimes. As an application or a solution becomes greater in size, the complexity becomes greater too. What we do not want is for the code to become complicated.

What's the difference between complex and complicated? Code is complex when it is written to sustainably deal with all the scenarios presented before it dynamically and understandably. Code is complicated when (in a complex solution) it is written in a way that handles every possible case based on static, very specific parameters (hard coding) and in a way that becomes difficult to understand, even for the person who wrote it.

I have seen a lot of it over my career; I wrote a lot of it at the beginning, too. It's a learning process and if you don't build good habits, you will fall into bad habits or fall back to a simpler solution for a more complex problem.

Once, when reviewing an old **Django** code base, I encountered an API written not in any API library but written using the **pandas data science library** with the ensuing result being presented using the Django `JSONResponse` function. It was baffling, and I couldn't help but think about why someone would write the code this way, until I found out that the person who had written it had had no previous web development expertise and was instead a data engineer. So, they reverted to what their vision of simplicity was: data science libraries, even for backend development.

Now, this slowed down the application immensely and, of course, had to be refactored, but – since we are blameless on individuals in this book – we couldn't blame the developer. We have to blame the habits that they fall back on and the simplicity they seek that eventually results in complicated code, when a slightly more complex yet concise solution would have resulted in better code.

Flat-nested/sparse-dense

The part about flat being better than nested, in particular, is a reason for those famous one-line Python codes that you see. Simple code shouldn't have to span across 20-30 lines when it can be done in a few. In a lot of languages, it cannot be done in a few lines, but in Python, it can.

Let's test out this concept when printing each value for this array: `my_list = [1,2,3,4,5]`:

Flat and sparse	Nested and dense
`print(*my_list)`	`for element in my_list: print(element)`

Table 2.1 – Flat and sparse versus nested and dense

Again, a very small example, but one of many present in the Python language. I recommend going through the list of libraries that Python comes pre-installed with; it is a very interesting read and will help you come up with a lot of ideas.

A lot of the time, this flat and sparse concept reduces the amount of code written by a significant amount. In turn, this makes the code more readable just from the reduced time it takes to read the code.

Let's dive into readability and the purity of the concept.

Readability-special cases-practicality-purity-errors

Python is meant to be a language that can be read and understood at some level by the layperson. It doesn't require any particularly special syntax and even the one-liners can be interpreted quite easily. Readability counts, and there are no special cases that are special enough to violate this credo. I have already expressed both philosophies through the previous examples, so there is no need to reiterate them here.

Practicality over purity is a fairly simple concept. Often, trying to follow best practices too strictly simply results in a waste of time. Sometimes, the best way to do something is to do it and then explain it later. However, in such cases, make sure that your boldness doesn't result in something that might break the system. In that case, **try-catch error handling** is your best friend. It also helps to pass errors silently when you need it to.

Balance between the two – progress and verification – results in code that has been verified and tested, but also code that is actually shipped to the end user. This balance is integral to any successful project. You have to be pragmatic when you are doing actual work, but you also have to realize that other people may not be so pragmatic in their actions and their estimates.

To take action in either direction, pragmatism or purity requires a sense of direction. It requires deciding something or some way and sticking to it.

Ambiguity/one way/Dutch

Anyone who has ever worked with clients knows how demoralizing and frustrating a vague requirement is. "*Do this, do that, we need this*" – that's all you hear, without any understanding from the other side or respect for how the process works. They have a certain goal in mind, and they don't care how you get there. That's fine for machines (and we'll learn how to do some of that), but for work done by people (and especially for coding work), that is not the way. You need to know exactly what is required so that you can do it precisely.

A lot of the time, even the clients don't know what they want; they have a vague idea that they want to act upon, but nothing beyond that. This ambiguity needs to be sorted out at the beginning of the project and it certainly should never spread to the code. Once something has been defined, then there is a way to do it that is the fastest, most secure, or most convenient (depending on requirements). This is the way that you need to find.

But, again, how do you find this way? It is not obvious to anyone who is not Dutch (a reference to the Dutch programmer Guido Van Rossum, the original author of Python). So, if you're Dutch, you're fine. If you're not, read this story (it's a much better fit for these principles than regular code):

Three friends were stranded on a boat with no food or water. These friends only had in their possession a lamp that seemed to be empty. One of the friends decided to rub the lamp, which caused a genie to appear. The genie granted each of the friends one wish since they had all summoned him together.

The first friend made his wish: "I wish to be sent to my wife and children." The wish was granted, and the friend disappeared, having been sent back to his family. The second friend wished to be sent back to his house in his hometown. This wish was similarly granted. The third friend, a loner, had nowhere he could think to go nor no one he could think to go to, so when his turn came, he said: "I wish I had my friends with me."

Now, this is an old story, but the way most people interpret it is that the friends were forcibly put back onto the boat by the third friend's wish: a classic tale of *be careful what you wish for*. However, an engineer can read the story and come up with some other possible scenarios. Maybe the third wish brought back more than those two people (if he had more than two friends); maybe it brought back no one (if the other two weren't considered friends, that would be a sad turn to the story), or it could even lead to an argument over what a friend is.

But most programming languages are like the genie. It does exactly what you tell it to do. If you're vague, the room you give it for interpretation can cost you, so be careful and only wish for the exact thing you want. And people (such as our previous clients) are like, well, the people. They sometimes know what they want, they sometimes do not. But, to succeed, they need to know precisely what they want in both the context of the goal (getting home) and the context of the rules that govern them (they could've let the third friend go first if they doubted his intentions). This is quite a conundrum, isn't it?

The key here – and this is something DevOps and **Agile methodologies** preach as well – is continuous improvement. Trying to continually find that one way. And if the scenario changes, tweaking the way to that scenario. This strategy is essential in coding, DevOps, machine learning, and practically every technology field. Iterative methodology helps turn even the vaguest goal into a bold mission statement and can provide unified direction.

The Dutch are a very direct people; only they could have invented a language as head-first as Python. Speaking of direct, you should probably read the next section now … or never, if you don't have the time right now (see what I did there?).

Now or never

This is another one of those principle pairs that is more about the method of writing than the writing itself. The statements of *now* being better than *never* but *never* being better than *right now* may seem somewhat paradoxical, but they describe the nature of writing code and delivering value through it.

Now doesn't mean *right this second*. It is meant to represent the near future and in that near future, the code we have written has delivered value. This is opposed to never releasing the code at all or releasing it in an unrealistically long timeframe, by the end of which the written code might become irrelevant. As Steve Jobs used to say:

Real artists ship.

However, *right now* is also never a good time. To release something too early, with no thought put into it, no understanding, and no game plan, can result in disaster. The basic lesson there is to look before you leap. And if you leap into a volcano, you probably didn't do your due diligence.

One of the reasons that *right now* is looked at as not a good time is because right now, there are no good ideas. There are never any good ideas right now; you kind of have to wait for your brain to come up with one. You push too hard trying to get something through that is hard to explain – that is a bad idea. That is how we can explain all the stupid trades that general managers make in sports at the trade deadline.

Hard-bad/easy-good

If you're having a hard time explaining something, it is probably a bad idea. There's not much to explain there – that's just common sense. A complex vision is no vision at all. It needs to be reduced, simplified, and shaped into something that most people can understand (or at least work toward).

An idea that is complicated is simply an idea that hasn't been reduced to its most useful, simplest component yet. As the old adage goes, there is always a ratio of 20% of the effort producing 80% of the output. To create the good idea, we just need to bring out and work on that 20%.

Namespaces

The lone zen, **namespaces** are just import statements written in ways that don't cause conflicts. In this example, there are two libraries, lib1 and lib2, both containing methods named example. What would be the solution that allows both of the methods to be imported into one Python file? You can just change one or both of their names to unique namespaces:

- Code without namespaces:

```
from lib1 import example
from lib2 import example
 This is bound to cause conflicts """
```

- Code with namespaces:

```
from lib1 import example as ex1
from lib2 import example as ex2
#This won't cause conflicts
```

A honking great idea indeed.

Through these principles, you can observe how Python has evolved into the language that it is and how it has distinguished itself from all the other programming languages. These changes have also helped make Python a language that aligns itself with DevOps principles. So, let's now observe the marriage between the principles behind Python and DevOps and how they are mutually beneficial to each other.

What Python offers DevOps

In the previous section, we focused on the principles of Python. Now, we are going to look into what following those principles offers DevOps as a practice and DevOps engineers in general. The principles behind DevOps and Python are more similar than they are different. They both share an emphasis on flexibility, automation, and conciseness. This makes Python and DevOps a perfect pairing in the field of DevOps. Even for DevOps professionals who may not have the sharpest coding skills, Python is easy to pick up, easy to use, and can be integrated with practically every tool and platform because almost all these platforms have native support and libraries in Python.

I previously stated that the reason that Python is so pervasive in DevOps is that it handles data that resides between curly brackets ({}) better than almost any other language. The offerings of Python for DevOps are numerous and will be covered in further detail in future chapters. Right now, we will go over some of these offerings in brief.

Operating systems

Python has native libraries that interact with the OS of any server that it is currently working on. These libraries allow for programmatic access to various OS processes. This is especially useful when you work with virtual machines on the cloud (such as with **Amazon EC2**). You can do things such as the following:

- Set environment variables in the OS
- Get information about files or directories
- Manipulate, create, or delete files and directories
- Kill or spawn processes and threads
- Create temporary files and file locations
- Run Bash scripts

OSs are nice and all, but they can be difficult to maintain in a desired state with ideal resource usage. For this challenge, we have a common solution in containerization.

Containerization

Containers are made using the **Docker** library. The creation, destruction, and modification of containers can be automated and orchestrated using Python. It provides a way to programmatically maintain and modify container states. Some applications include the following:

- Interaction with Docker API for commands, such as getting a list of Docker containers or images present in the OS
- Automatically generating **Docker Compose files** from a list of Docker images
- Building Docker images
- Orchestrating containers using the **Kubernetes library**
- Testing and verifying Docker images

You may be wondering what the point of containers is, and that may be because you've never gotten tired of the constant online discourse over OSs and frameworks and which ones are superior (in fact, you may have even encouraged such malarkey). But, containers exist for those who tire of such debate and instead want isolated environments for all their specific operating needs. So they made one with containers, and someone had the bright idea to call them microservices.

Microservices

Sometimes, containers and **microservices** are used interchangeably, but in modern DevOps that is not necessarily the case. Yes, it is containers that make microservices possible, but t the overall writing of microservices on top of those containers is efficient code that has the most bang for its buck. Some reasons for Python use in microservices are as follows:

- Strong native library support inside of a Python container – libraries such as **json**, **asyncio**, and **subprocess**
- Excellent native code modules that simplify certain iterative and manipulative operations on data such as the `collection` module
- Ability to properly natively handle semi-structured and varied JSON data that is usually used in microservices

To have these microservices interact with each other effectively and consistently, we need some repetition, some consistent repetition. What's the word I'm looking for ... automaton ... no, that's a robot ... autograph ... no, that'll be what I do once this book becomes a bestseller ... automation, yes, that's the word. Automation.

Automation is probably the primary selling point for DevOps engineers when it comes to Python because of its incredible **automation library** and support features. Most systems guys who transition to DevOps prefer their precious **Bash scripting**, and that does have a place in environments such as these, but Python is more powerful and more flexible, and it is better supported by the community and the companies in the industry overall. Some applications of Python for automation in this case would be the following:

- Various **Software Development Kits** (**SDKs**) for cloud-based deployments in **AWS**, **Azure**, **Google Cloud**, and other providers
- Support for automated building and testing of applications
- Support for monitoring applications and sending notifications
- Support for parsing and scraping necessary data from web pages, databases, and various other sources of data

Now that we have talked the talk, let's walk a little. A light jog to combine Python and DevOps.

A couple of simple DevOps tasks in Python

I have so far preached to you the virtues of DevOps and the virtues of Python but so far, I have shown you very little of how the two work together. Now, we get to that part. Here, I will demonstrate a couple of examples of how to use Python to automate some regular DevOps tasks that some engineers may have to perform on a daily basis. These two examples will be from AWS, though they are applicable in other big clouds as well and can be applied on most data center servers if you have the right APIs.

The code for this chapter and all future chapters are stored in this repository: `https://github.com/PacktPublishing/Hands-On-Python-for-DevOps`

Automated shutdown of a server

Oftentimes, there is the case of certain servers that only need to be up during working hours and then need to be switched off afterward. Now, this particular scenario has a lot of caveats, which include the platform used, the accounts where the servers are running, and how working hours are measured… but for this scenario, we are simply going to shut our EC2 servers down in an AWS account using an **AWS Lambda** function microservice that runs a Python script that leverages the **boto3 library**. That sounds like a lot? Let's break it down.

In my AWS account, I have two EC2 instances running. Every second that they run costs me money. However, I need them during business hours. Here they are:

Figure 2.2 – Running instances

Creatively named, I know. But they are running, and there will come a point in time when I want them to not be running. So, to achieve that, I need to find some way to stop them. I could stop them one by one, but that's tedious. And would I still do that if these 2 instances were 1,000 instances? No. So, we need to find another way.

We could try the **command-line interface** (**CLI**), but this is a coding book and not a CLI book, so we won't. Though, keep it in mind if you want to try it. So, let's look to our old friend Python, and also to a service that allows you to deploy a function that you can call at any time, called AWS Lambda. Here are the steps to create a Lambda function and use it to start and stop an EC2 instance:

1. Let's create a function called `stopper` with the latest available Python runtime (3.10 for this book):

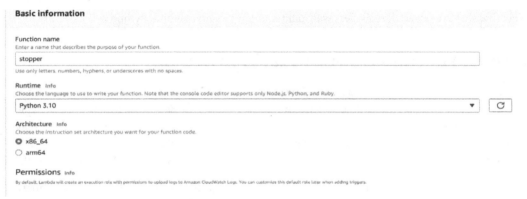

Figure 2.3 – Creating a Lambda function

2. Next, you will either have to create an execution role for the Lambda function or give it an existing one. This will be important later. But for now, do the one you prefer. Click **Create function** to create your new blank canvas.

    The reason we are using the AWS environment for the microservices to manipulate EC2 instances (other than the obvious reasons) is that the runtime that they provide comes with the `boto3` library by default, which is very useful for resource interaction.

3. Before we can start or stop any instance, we need to list them out. You have to load and dump the return function once to handle the `datetime` data type. For now, let's just initialize the `boto3` client for EC2 and try and list all of the instances that are currently available:

```
import boto3
import json

def lambda_handler(event, context):
    """Initialize EC2 Client"""
    ec2_client = boto3.client('ec2')
    """Return JSON"""
    return(json.loads(json.dumps(ec2_client.describe_instances(),default=str)))
```

Figure 2.4 – Initial code to describe instances

Running this with a test will get you an exception thrown similar to this:

```
Response
{
  "errorMessage": "An error occurred (UnauthorizedOperation) when calling the DescribeInstances operation: You are not authorized to perform this operation.",
  "errorType": "ClientError",
  "requestId": "ad9a99e8-755a-49ba-8633-16112ccaa971",
  "stackTrace": [
```

Figure 2.5 – Authorization exception

That is because the Lambda function also has an **identity and access management** (**IAM**) role, and that role does not have the required permissions to describe the instances. So, let's set the permissions that we may need.

4. As shown in the following figure, under **Configuration | Permissions**, you will find the role assigned to the Lambda function:

Figure 2.6 – Finding the role for permissions

5. On the page for the role, go to **Add permissions** and then **Attach policies**:

Figure 2.7 – Attaching a permission

Let's give the Lambda function full access to the EC2 services since we will need it to stop the instance as well. If you prefer or if you feel that's too much access, you can make a custom role:

Figure 2.8 – Attaching the appropriate permission

6.   Let's run this again and see the results:

Response

```
{
  "Reservations": [
    {
      "Groups": [],
      "Instances": [
        {
          "AmiLaunchIndex": 0,
          "ImageId": "ami-05548f9cecf47b442",
          "InstanceId": "i-05bee5e10e42445cd",
          "InstanceType": "t2.micro",
          "KeyName": "wordpresssitekeypair",
          "LaunchTime": "2023-07-26 09:57:18+00:00",
          "Monitoring": {
            "State": "disabled"
          },
          "Placement": {
            "AvailabilityZone": "us-east-1b",
            "GroupName": "",
            "Tenancy": "default"
          },
          "PrivateDnsName": "ip-172-31-27-120.ec2.internal",
          "PrivateIpAddress": "172.31.27.120",
          "ProductCodes": [],
          "PublicDnsName": "ec2-52-90-0-226.compute-1.amazonaws.com",
          "PublicIpAddress": "52.90.0.226",
          "State": {
            "Code": 16,
            "Name": "running"
          },
          "StateTransitionReason": "",
          "SubnetId": "subnet-0a534512db1399d05",
          "VpcId": "vpc-02f72269afe1155dd",
          "Architecture": "x86_64",
          "BlockDeviceMappings": [
            {
```

Figure 2.9 – Successful code run

You'll see the display of instances as well as information regarding whether they are running or not.

7. Now, let's get to the part where we shut down the running instances. Add code to filter among the instances for ones that are running and get a list of their IDs, which we will use to reference the instances we want to stop:

```python
import boto3
import json

def lambda_handler(event, context):
    """Initialize EC2 Client"""
    ec2_client = boto3.client('ec2')
    """Get running instances"""
    instances_json = json.loads(json.dumps(ec2_client.describe_instances(Filters = [
        {
            'Name':'instance-state-name',
            'Values':[
                'running'
            ]
        }
    ]),
    default=str))
    """Filter to only instance_ids"""
    instance_ids = [instance["Instances"][0]["InstanceId"] for instance in instances_json["Reservations"]]
    """Shut down selected instance_ids"""
    response = ec2_client.stop_instances(
        InstanceIds=instance_ids
    )
    return response
```

Figure 2.10 – Adding code that stops the instances

Simple enough to understand, especially if we are following the principle of readability and explicitness.

The instances are now in a state where they are shutting down. And soon, they will be stopped:

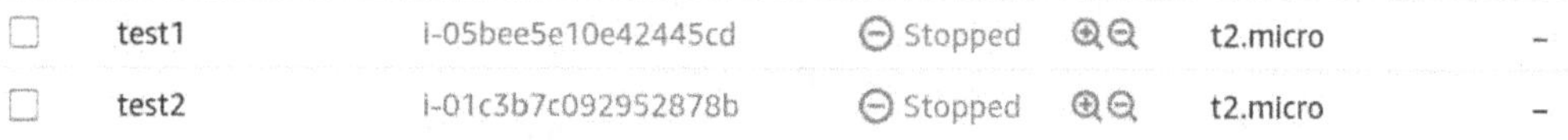

| ☐ | test1 | i-05bee5e10e42445cd | ⊖ Stopped | ⊕ ⊖ | t2.micro | – |
| ☐ | test2 | i-01c3b7c092952878b | ⊖ Stopped | ⊕ ⊖ | t2.micro | – |

Figure 2.11 – Shut down instances

8. Now that we have done it once, let's automate it further by using a service called EventBridge, which can trigger that function every day. Navigate to **Amazon EventBridge** and make an EventBridge schedule:

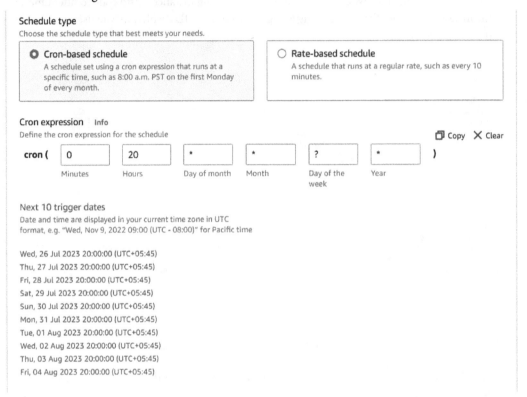

Figure 2.12 – Setting up a cron job on EventBridge

9.   Select our Lambda function as the event target:

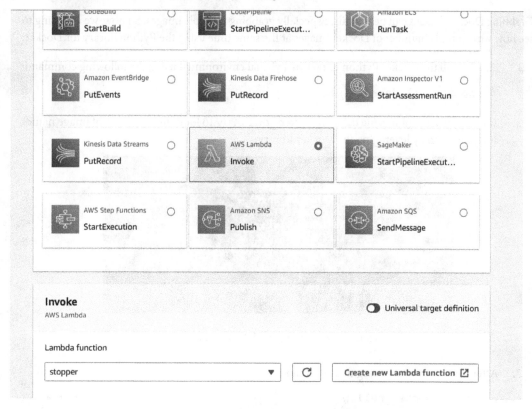

Figure 2.13 – Selecting Lambda to invoke for EventBridge

You can now create the EventBridge scheduled event, which will trigger at 8 P.M. every day and list and shut down your EC2 instances.

So, in following these steps, you now have the tools necessary to schedule the shutdown of instances based on the timed schedule that you want.

Autopull a list of Docker images

Grabbing Docker images can be tedious. Especially grabbing multiple images. So now, we are going to see how we can pull a number of Docker images at the same time using the Python library for Docker:

1. First, install the Docker Python library in a virtual environment using the following command:

    ```
    pip install docker
    ```

2. Then, write a script in a file called `docker_pull.py` to loop through a list of image names and pull them by leveraging the Docker library:

```python
import docker

def pull_docker_images():
        client = docker.from_env()
        image_list = ["redis:latest", "nginx:latest"]
        for image in image_list:
                print("Pulling image {}".format(image))
                client.images.pull(image)

if __name__ == "__main__":
        pull_docker_images()
```

Figure 2.14 – Code to pull Docker images

3. After this, run the file using this command:

    ```
    python docker_pull.py
    ```

    You can then run the `docker images` command to check out the Docker containers that you may have locally:

```
REPOSITORY                          TAG        IMAGE ID        CREATED         SIZE
redis                               latest     7e89539dd8bd    2 weeks ago     130MB
nginx                               latest     021283c8eb95    3 weeks ago     187MB
```

Figure 2.15 – List of Docker images

So, this gives you a pretty nifty way to get the Docker containers you want with the tags that you want on them.

Summary

Python is not just about writing code; it is about a coding philosophy – a philosophy that has made Python incredibly popular among DevOps engineers. The writing of the Zen of Python affected the way that the language was developed, and we still see the consequences today in both Python and DevOps. Python's philosophy offers the DevOps realm the programming language that fits its philosophy.

Python has numerous uses that facilitate a lot of DevOps tasks. So, hopefully, this chapter has given you some insights into what makes Python such a good companion for DevOps. In the next chapter, you will see that companionship in action and learn how to use your knowledge in a truly hands-on way.

The Simplest Ways to Start Using DevOps in Python Immediately

Things don't just happen. They are made to happen.

– John F. Kennedy

Over the past couple of chapters, you've probably been thinking, all these principles and philosophies are fine, but I want to get my hands dirty! If that's what you want, then this is the chapter for you. In this chapter, you will learn how to use Python and its libraries to serve the purposes of your workloads.

Now, I'm not suggesting that you switch to Python-based alternatives from what you are currently using. In fact, most of the tools and techniques that we are about to discuss are meant to be in support of existing infrastructure and methods as opposed to a replacement for them.

This chapter is meant to give you a good grasp of the possibilities that the Python programming language provides DevOps as well as the ways that you can integrate it into your pre-existing systems and infrastructure.

In this chapter, we are going to learn about a few simple implementations of Python in different aspects of API calls:

- Making API calls and the different ways that API calls are made

- How Python can help analyze, construct, and optimize your workload's networking resources

Technical requirements

There are a few technical requirements that may need to be fulfilled if you want to get the most out of this chapter:

- A GitHub account

- A Replit account (which has a single sign-on with GitHub)

- A Hugging Face account

- A Google account

- Any computing device with an internet connection and a command line interface

- The ability to tolerate my writing style

Well, if you can get those in hand, then you are ready to start your journey in this chapter. Let's get going.

Introducing API calls

To define API calls, let's start with what an **Application Programming Interface** (**API**) is. An API is a software interface that offers your application access to functions and processes from other applications. Think of it like this: when a user tries to get information from an application, they do so through the **user interface** (**UI**). The API has a similar function for software, so you could call API the UI of software.

Now, API calls are made for a number of reasons:

- You don't want to write the underlying logic for a big feature yourself (trust me, a lot of the time, you don't).

- The API gives access to resources that you ordinarily would not have (i.e., creating a Virtual Machine using the API of a cloud provider)

- You just want to get some information into your application (public APIs are very good for this)

Any coding library that you use for code is technically an API. You pull the library in and you call it to perform a function for your application. So, you can see why the definition of APIs can be confusing sometimes. But the point is this: more things are APIs than are not APIs. Everything you see in an app or a website comes from APIs.

So, let's dive into a couple of examples of how to use APIs to our benefit in DevOps.

Exercise 1 – calling a Hugging Face Transformer API

I chose this exercise because it is free, it will introduce you to a lot of integral tools and concepts behind APIs, and **Hugging Face APIs** are quite popular, so you will get hands-on experience with those. The API that we will be using specifically is a transformer that turns a written prompt into an image. It's a great API to learn and find out how APIs in general work. For this lesson, I am using a Google Colab notebook, which is a Jupyter Notebook hosted by Google. It's pretty useful when you want to recreate runtimes for certain sections of code. It's like having your own little test section that you can divide into even smaller sections if you want to. Let's make a notebook to further explore our Hugging Face API:

1. To open a Colab notebook, you can go to `colab.research.google.com` and create a new notebook. The end result should be something like this:

Figure 3.1 – Initial notebook created with Google Colab

2. The first thing we need to do is install the correct libraries. These libraries contain the functions and modules with which we call our APIs. You can install them directly in the notebook if you'd like. We are going to install the `huggingface_hub` and `transformers[agents]` libraries. Here is the command for this:

```
!pip install huggingface_hub transformers[agents]
```

When you put this command in the cell and press play, it will install the libraries in your runtime:

Figure 3.2 – Installing required libraries

3. The next thing that you need to do is log in to `huggingface_hub` using an API key.

    This is where the concept of the API key comes from. An API key is like a login but for your software. Most companies only allow full access to their APIs through the purchase of an API key. A lot of open source projects such as Hugging Face have API keys to promote and track user interaction and sometimes upgrade their users to a premium version if they want.

4. To get a Hugging Face API key, you must first go to the `huggingface.co` web page and sign up or log in if you've already signed up. After doing that, go to your profile and then to the **Settings** tab and into the **Access Tokens** tab from there. You can generate an access token for use there:

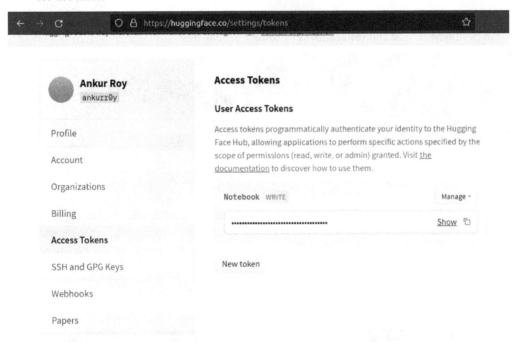

Figure 3.3 – Generating an access token for the Hugging Face API

5. You can copy this token for use in your next section of code. Here, you import the Hugging Face login module for the login API, and you input your key to use the API:

```
from huggingface_hub import login
login("<your_key_here>")
```

You'll get this message if you've loaded it correctly. If so, congratulations, you successfully called the login API:

```
Token will not been saved to git credential helper. Pass `add_to_git_credential=True` if you want to set the git credential as well.
Token is valid (permission: write).
Your token has been saved to /root/.cache/huggingface/token
Login successful
```

Figure 3.4 – Successful login and initialization

Now comes the fun part. We are going to use the Hugging Face Transformer API to take a line of text and turn it into an image. But first, we must import a Hugging Face agent using the HfAgent API (see the pattern?):

```
from transformers import HfAgent
agent = HfAgent("https://api-inference.huggingface.co/models/
bigcode/starcoderbase")
```

We are using the starcoderbase model for this. Once you run this and get the agent, you can simply type in a prompt to generate an image:

```
agent.run("Draw me a picture of `prompt`", prompt="rainbow
butterflies")
```

But remember, if you don't want to wait half an hour for your image, use the GPU runtime by going to the **runtime** tab and selecting it:

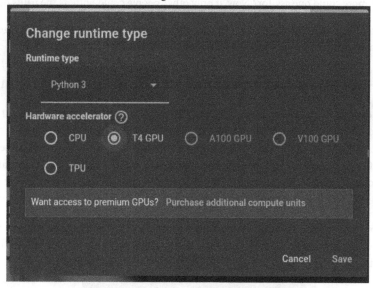

Figure 3.5 – Choosing a GPU for faster image processing

6. The end product will leave you shocked and satisfied. You'll get something like this:

Figure 3.6 – Your final result (beautiful, isn't it?)

So, we have completed this exercise and successfully called an API that has given us a visibly satisfying conclusion. What more could one ask for? Now, if only other people could witness the fruits of your labor!

Well, that's what calling APIs is all about. APIs are meant to be consumed by your target audience and so now, we are going to see how we can distribute our APIs.

Exercise 2 – creating and releasing an API for consumption

Deploying applications is one of the most frequent tasks that a DevOps engineer might encounter. It is important to have a good, fast deployment, but before that, it is important to have a deployment in the first place. Deploying smaller and larger applications are alike in a lot of ways. One major way in which they differ is the lengths you must go through to maintain availability on larger applications. We won't be discussing that in this section. We will instead just try to get an API up for adding two numbers. Like I said, let's keep it simple and begin creating a new **Replit Repl** and start coding in it.

1. Sign up for an account at `replit.com`. You can create small virtual environments for practically every application framework and code base there. Once you have signed up, you can create a **Repl**, which is a small virtual server, by clicking the **Create Repl** button:

Figure 3.7 – Button to create a Repl

2. Once you have done that, search for and create a Repl with the **Flask** template. The name is not relevant:

Figure 3.8 – Initializing a Flask Repl

This will give you an IDE that contains boilerplate Flask code that is pre-initialized and installed with the basic Flask libraries:

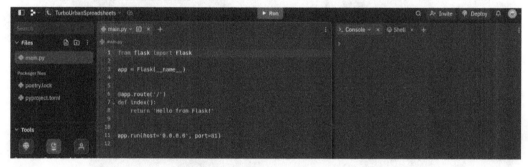

Figure 3.9 – Initial Flask framework

3. Concerning the preceding figure, when you click the **Run** button shown on top, you'll launch a Flask server, a URL that will return some sort of answer when it is called. The server's default route of " / " has already been defined. So, if you open the URL in a new tab, you'll get something like this:

Hello from Flask!

Figure 3.10 – Initial Flask web page

This function just returns a string on a webpage. Typically, APIs are written in a JSON format. So, let's turn this into JSON. In Flask, that is pretty easy. You can just pass a variable that is a dictionary in the return type:

```
1   from flask import Flask
2
3   app = Flask(__name__)
4
5
6   @app.route('/')
7 ᵛ def index():
8     returning_json_value = {"Mic":"Check"}
9     return returning_json_value
10
11
12  app.run(host='0.0.0.0', port=81)
```

Figure 3.11 – Writing a simple JSON API in Flask

Once that's done, you'll get a return value in JSON:

Figure 3.12 – JSON API result

4. This API, as it is, only returns static values. To have it take user input, simply add `request` parameters in the URL itself. Let's modify our application to take two parameters, `num1` and `num2`, which will be added, and their sums shown in the JSON return value:

```
    main.py
1   from flask import Flask, request
2
3   app = Flask(__name__)
4
5
6   @app.route('/')
7 ᵛ def index():
8     num1 = request.args.get("num1")
9     num2 = request.args.get("num2")
10    returning_json_value = {"Sum of parameters":int(num1) +
    int(num2)}
11    return returning_json_value
12
13
14  app.run(host='0.0.0.0', port=81)
15
```

Figure 3.13 – Flask API code to add two numbers

The end result requires a URL in the form of `<your_url_here>/?num1=<number>&num2=<number>`. The result would look something like this:

Figure 3.14 – Flask API call to add two numbers

So, now you have learned how to make an API in Python that adds two numbers and deploys the API. That's a really big step. The only thing that gets exponentially more complex in the programming world is business logic. Security and networking are important too, but they usually follow a set formula. As long as you can deploy your logic to your end user, you're good.

Now, that you have learned the art of the API, we are going to dive into what delivers APIs to their end users. We are diving into networking. Networking is such an integral part of DevOps and application development in general that sometimes it's not mentioned at all. So, let's look at a few useful ways that we can use Python on the networking side.

Networking

No, this is not about growing your LinkedIn connections, although that's something I'd recommend doing too. Computer networks are essential to the functioning of every application these days because they are the only way to deliver constant value to the user while keeping them connected to your environment. Almost every device these days is connected to a network, which is why understanding the network of devices and the network of networks (it's something called the internet, ever heard of it?) is very important.

I am now going to demonstrate two examples of how to use Python for networking insights and data collection.

Exercise 1 – using Scapy to sniff packets and visualize packet size over time

Scapy is a Python library that can be used to replicate, simulate, and manipulate the data packets that are sent over a computer network. Scapy is a very useful tool in the belt of any developer or DevOps professional.

In this exercise, we are going to use Scapy to collect a list of packets and get their timestamps and packet sizes. We are then going to map these onto a chart that we make using the **matplotlib library**. You can use the previously mentioned Google Colab for this exercise. So, let's initialize the notebook and start writing our code:

1. First, we need to install the `matplotlib` and `scapy` libraries:

```
!pip install scapy matplotlib
```

2. Now, let's write the code to use Scapy's `sniff` module to get a list of packet sizes over timestamps:

```python
from scapy.all import sniff

# Lists to store packet sizes and timestamps
packet_sizes = []
timestamps = []

#Handle packets and get the necessary data
def packet_handler(packet):
print(packet)
packet_sizes.append(len(packet))
timestamps.append(packet.time)

# Start packet sniffing on the default network interface
sniff(prn=packet_handler, count=100)
```

You will get a list of the length of the last 100 packets that went through your network along with the timestamp and the type of traffic. If you refer to the following diagram, the packet sizes are stored in the `packet_sizes` array and the timestamps of the packet are stored in the `timestamps` variable:

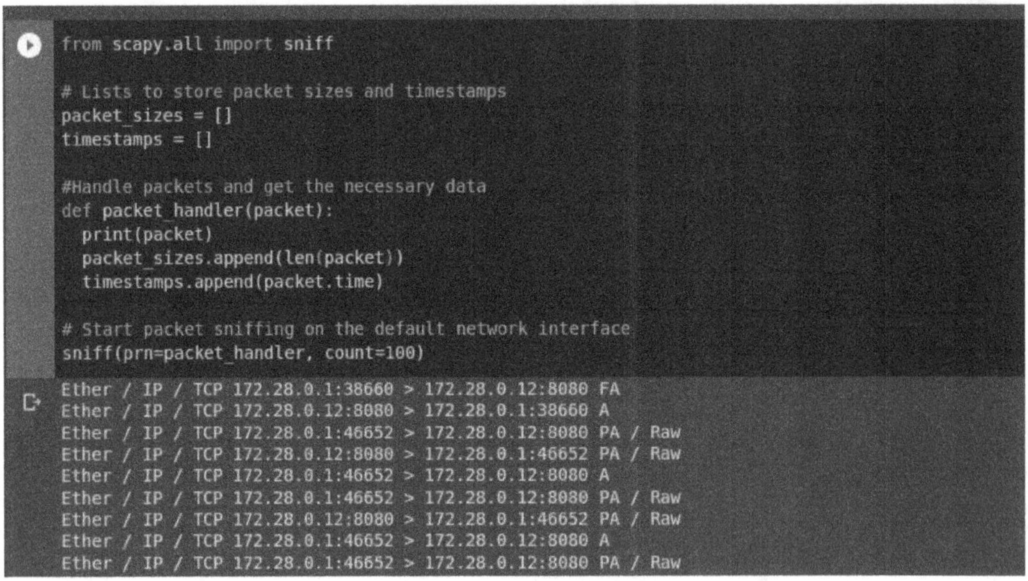

Figure 3.15 – Sniffing packets in your computing device

3. Let's now write the code to plot the packet size over time using `matplotlib`:

```
# Create a plot
plt.figure(figsize=(16, 8))
plt.plot(timestamps, packet_sizes, marker='o')
plt.xlabel("Time")
plt.ylabel("Packet Size")
plt.title("Packet Size over Time")
plt.grid(True)
plt.show()
```

This will give us a chart with time on the *x*-axis and packet size on the *y*-axis:

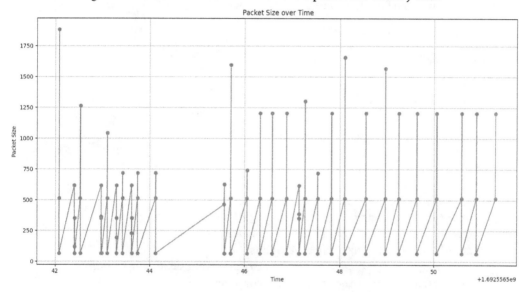

Figure 3.16 – Chart of packet size over time

The preceding chart shows a pattern of network activity that seems to involve several correlated packets. So, you can see the network analysis library coming in handy already.

So, we have now tracked our network activity and generated data insights from it using Python. Let's look at one more network implementation, this time focusing on the routing rules that your device (or the device you are running your workload on) has.

Exercise 2 – generating a routing table for your device

Routing tables define the routes that certain web traffic takes within your devices. These tables exist in practically every device, and they define the routes by which those devices access computer networks. You can use the **netifaces Python library** to generate a routing table showing all the available routes and destinations that your device contains. The netifaces library in this case is used to collect the network interfaces (hence the name *netifaces*) of your operating system. You will then parse this information and display it in a tabular form. You can once again use Google Colab for this, though for more interesting results, you could try running the code locally.

1. Let's begin the steps to generate a routing table for your device. If you've been following along so far, you know the first step is installing the library:

    ```
    !pip install netifaces
    ```

2. Next, write code to generate the routing table:

    ```
    #import library
    import netifaces
    #begin function
    def generate_routing_table():
    routing_table = []
    #Loop through network interfaces
    for interface in netifaces.interfaces():
        #initialize current address of interface
    Interface_addresses =netifaces.ifaddresses(interface)
    #Check for, then loop through the addresses
    if netifaces.AF_INET in addresses:
    for entry in        interface_addresses[netifaces.AF_INET]:
        #Create routing entry wherefound
    if 'netmask' in entry and 'addr' in     entry:
    routing_entry = {
    'interface': interface,
    'destination': entry['addr'],
    'netmask': entry['netmask']
    }
    #Append route to routing table
    routing_table.append(routing_entry)
    return routing_table

    #Call function
    routing_table = generate_routing_table()
    #Display routing table
    for entry in routing_table:
    print(f"Interface: {entry['interface']}")
    ```

```
print(f"Destination: {entry['destination']}")
print(f"Netmask: {entry['netmask']}")
print("-" * 30)
```

It's a lot of code, but fairly easy to make sense of. It also provides you with detailed information about where the network traffic goes from your network interfaces. If you tried it on Colab as I suggested, you'd get something like this:

```
Interface: lo
Destination: 127.0.0.1
Netmask: 255.0.0.0
-------------------------------
Interface: eth0
Destination: 172.28.0.12
Netmask: 255.255.0.0
-------------------------------
```

Figure 3.17 – Route table on Colab

And if you've done it on your personal computer, you might get something like this:

```
Interface: lo
Destination: 127.0.0.1
Netmask: 255.0.0.0
-------------------------------
Interface: wlp3s0
Destination: 192.168.0.176
Netmask: 255.255.255.0
-------------------------------
Interface: br-46b7f7078ecd
Destination: 172.18.0.1
Netmask: 255.255.0.0
-------------------------------
Interface: br-787b4d9e4240
Destination: 172.19.0.1
Netmask: 255.255.0.0
-------------------------------
Interface: docker0
Destination: 172.17.0.1
Netmask: 255.255.0.0
-------------------------------
```

Figure 3.18 – Route table on a personal computer

A bit more baggage was added there.

But that is the gist of it, and these are just a couple of ways you can use Python to facilitate the networking aspect of DevOps.

Summary

In this chapter, you learned a thing or two about the hands-on part of this book. You've learned about APIs and computer networks, which practically means you're halfway there as far as the Python DevOps implementation goes.

In this chapter, not only did you learn about these important DevOps concepts, but you also learned how you can implement them in your DevOps process. You can take this code and implement it directly in your DevOps workload right now if that benefits you.

These fundamentals that you have learned will help you enhance, monitor, and diagnose problems on practically any DevOps workload that you may encounter. In the next chapter, we will discuss the creation of resources in a DevOps workload and how and where Python can be of assistance in the process.

4

Provisioning Resources

Life is chaotic, dangerous, and surprising. Buildings should reflect that.

– Frank Gehry (famous architect)

DevOps is a game of resources. Of taking the resources that you have and putting them in the right place. It sounds easy, but it is not. The acquisition of resources is based on several criteria and requirements that the DevOps engineer receives. If you want to optimally provision resources, then you have to understand the logic and reasoning behind provisioning those resources as well as the strategy behind the intended use of the underlying infrastructure.

And if you want all that in plain English: take only what you need.

So, that will be one of the underlying concepts of this chapter: rightsizing. **Rightsizing** is the art of finding the optimal resource sizes for your application or workload. A lot of this is just trial and error (often yours, but someone else's if you can get it) and trust me when I say this, it is much easier to do that programmatically than manually in the modern DevOps landscape.

But that's easier said than done, because sometimes the load placed upon your resources is a lot larger than the size of the resources you've provisioned, especially if your application becomes popular. You become a victim of your own success. Or you provision resources that can hold at maximum capacity, but that capacity is only occasional, and you can't possibly ramp your resources up in time.

This brings us to the second underlying concept of this chapter: scaling. **Scaling** your resources up and down is one of the important aspects of DevOps and removing resources is as key an aspect of provisioning them as adding resources is. This must almost always be done programmatically, and we will look at a couple of ways in which Python can help us with that.

If you master these concepts and how to use them effectively, you can save you and your organization a massive amount of time, money, and resources. In addition to this, you will be able to deliver on spikes in demand in a way that addresses the needs of both your organization and its customers.

In this chapter, we will explore the following:

- How to provision virtual resources with Python
- How to use Python SDKs for various clouds and provision resources through them
- How scaling works, the types of scaling, and choosing the correct type of scaling
- How containerization of resources can help with rightsizing and easier provisioning (and where Python plays a role)

Technical requirements

Here is a list of requirements that you will need to meet to complete the exercises in this chapter:

- Python installation with boto3, Kubernetes, and Docker libraries installed
- An AWS account
- Knowledge of how to use a Jupyter Notebook
- If you are on Windows, the use of **Windows Subsystem for Linux** (WSL) to use Docker locally
- A GitHub account, and basic knowledge of Git and repositories
- Access to this book's repository: `https://github.com/PacktPublishing/Hands-On-Python-for-DevOps`
- A basic understanding of virtualization and Kubernetes

Python SDKs (and why everyone uses them)

Let's take it from the top. **SDKs**, or **software development kits**, are official programming libraries and **CLIs** released by a platform that allows developers to develop tools and applications that leverage that platform. These SDKs are usually written in very popular languages so as to cover the largest number of developers possible.

The three major clouds (where the majority of DevOps work is done) have the following programming languages in common among them for SDKs: **Java**, **.NET**, **C++**, **Go**, **JavaScript/TypeScript/Node.js**, and **Python**. If you work on one of these – and the chances that you do are greater than the chances that you don't – you need to choose a programming language.

So, the question then becomes, why Python? Also, why are we asking this question four chapters into this book? Well, I'll tell you. Python is the exact balance between loose and structured that is necessary to pull off a lot of DevOps principles.

Strictly typed languages such as Java, .NET, and C++ can be good for development, but they will produce awful results for the flexibility that is required of the modern DevOps workload. That being said, most clouds are built on these languages. But operating on them is a different game entirely. Think of these languages as the bones that provide sturdiness and Python as the joints that provide flexibility – they should be everywhere that requires flexibility.

Then, on the other end of the spectrum, you have that JavaScript trio. The reason they are sometimes unsuited for this – even though there is a massive amount of support for them from the major clouds – is the limitations and syntactic quirks that are natural to these languages. They aren't meant to natively work this way and in addition to that, they are single-threaded and difficult to operate concurrently.

The primary competitor and, at times, cooperator to Python in this department is Go. And let me tell you, Go is good. A majority of cloud-based tools such as **Docker** and **Kubernetes** are built in Go, and ones that aren't are usually built in Python. But Go is really the only other language that can go toe to toe with Python for how useful it is in DevOps. And I'm telling you this because much of what I'm going to work through in this chapter will involve frameworks written in Go, such as **Terraform** and Docker.

With all of this information out of the way, let's finally put the focus back on Python. Python is easygoing. It has variable assignment without strict data types, which is incredibly useful for loosely coupled services, a very common architectural choice. It has a big community and is almost always the first SDK offered by modern infrastructure providers. As mentioned previously in this section, Python can essentially enter into a symbiotic relationship with any framework written in any language. If there is a popular framework or tool, its Pythonic version will likely be well-maintained and properly updated.

That was a quick look at the importance of and popularity of Python SDKs, now, we are now going to see an example of how Python SDKs can be used to provision resources.

Creating an AWS EC2 instance with Python's boto3 library

Boto3 – it's a name you've probably heard very often if you've worked with AWS and Python. It is the SDK that contains nearly every major AWS service that is currently available with Python.

For this example, we are going to use Boto3 in a script that will provision an EC2 instance in your AWS account. It sounds simple, but there are still a lot of steps that you need to follow to make it happen, so let's get started. We will now begin by first logging into our AWS account and searching for the Sagemaker service. Let's dive into it:

1. For this exercise, we need a clean environment where we can write Python code but also configure permissions in a terminal. To do this, in my AWS account, I'm going to create something else that we will use down the line: a **Sagemaker** notebook. A Sagemaker notebook is a Jupyter notebook service run on AWS servers:

Amazon SageMaker > Notebook instances > **Create notebook instance**

Create notebook instance

Amazon SageMaker provides pre-built fully managed notebook instances that run Jupyter notebooks. The notebook instances include example code for common model training and hosting exercises. Learn more ⬀

Notebook instance settings

Notebook instance name

```
Book
```

Maximum of 63 alphanumeric characters. Can include hyphens (-), but not spaces. Must be unique within your account in an AWS Region.

Notebook instance type

```
ml.t3.medium                                                    ▼
```

Elastic Inference Learn more ⬀

```
ml.eia1.medium                                                  ▼
```

Platform identifier Learn more ⬀

Figure 4.1 – Console to create a notebook instance in Amazon Sagemaker

If you look at the breadcrumb at the top, you can see that the path is **Amazon Sagemaker** -> **Notebook instances** -> **Create notebook instance**.

2. Any smaller notebook is good. We're using **ml.t3.medium** for this exercise:

	Name ▽	Instance	Creation time ▼	Status ▽	Actions
○	notebook	ml.t3.medium	9/20/2023, 1:02:02 AM	⊘ InService	Open Jupyter | Open JupyterLab

Figure 4.2 – Created notebook

Once your notebook is up and running, click on **Open Jupyter** to get to your **Jupyter IDE**. Now, the instance itself will have some AWS permissions because it is an AWS creation, but not enough to provision an EC2 programmatically. It will, however, come pre-installed with boto3 and the **AWS CLI**.

Important note

If you don't have them installed, install `boto3` with `pip` and the AWS CLI through AWS's official website (`https://docs.aws.amazon.com/cli/latest/userguide/getting-started-install.html`), which contains installers for all operating systems.

---

3. Now, let's try and provision the EC2 with the pre-existing Sagemaker role that comes pre-assigned to Sagemaker:

```
[7]: import boto3

     ec2_client = boto3.resource("ec2", region_name="us-west-2")
     ec2_client.create_instances(ImageId="ami-002829755fa238bfa",InstanceType="t2.micro", MaxCount=1, MinCount=1)

[7]: [ec2.Instance(id='i-0ac2297825155b786')]

[ ]:
```

Figure 4.3 – Code to invoke boto3 API

It worked. But, as you see here, the Sagemaker instance already came pre-configured with a role that had EC2 access.. If that had not been the case, you would have had to give the role some permissions or use the AWS CLI to attach a role profile to the instance. But it worked, and that is great. You can view your EC2 instance in your AWS console.

However, there are a few things to note here:

- You always need to define an ImageID (AWS has a public catalog). The one I'm using is AWS's proprietary Linux version.

- You need to define the instance size and the maximum and minimum number of instances to create.

Now, that was simple and easy to understand, wasn't it? Well, that's good. Now we can move on to the concepts that make the provisioning of resources so necessary. Scaling and autoscaling are essential concepts in DevOps and they are both just a matter of provisioning resources.

Scaling and autoscaling

Scaling is the act of increasing or decreasing the size of a workload or resource depending on the demand for it. **Autoscaling** is doing this automatically based on some sort of trigger.

As is often the case with workloads and applications, you can become a victim of your own success. The more your application succeeds, the greater the strain on it due to demand from users or services. To manage this strain often requires limitations placed on access to your application. You should do this if you don't want to get overwhelmed with requests, trust me, because someone will try to do exactly that. But you should also have provisions in your infrastructure that can help it grow naturally with your growing user base.

That is where scaling comes in. Scaling can be done either vertically (adding greater computing power to a device) or horizontally (adding more computers). When performing one powerful act, vertical scaling is ideal and when processing a greater number of requests, you'll need horizontal scaling. Most DevOps workloads require the latter over the former.

We will now explore the different types of scaling based on how hands-on you have to be with the workload that you are scaling. We will start with manual scaling and slowly escalate toward a more automated approach.

Manual scaling with Python

Before we dive into autoscaling, let's just look at some regular scaling (done with Python, of course). We will vertically scale an instance manually using Python's SDK for AWS. I will be using just my regular local IDE. But you can do this with any combination of Python, AWS CLI, and an AWS account. So, let's head into the steps you would need to take to manually scale an EC2 instance using Python scripts:

1. Here is the code to create an EC2 instance (this will be up in the book's repository as well):

```python
import boto3

def create_ec2():
    ec2_client = boto3.resource("ec2")
    print(ec2_client.create_instances(ImageId="ami-051f7e7f6c2f40dc1",
                                       InstanceType="t2.nano", MaxCount=1, MinCount=1))

if __name__ == "__main__":
    create_ec2()
```

Figure 4.4 – Function to create an EC2 instance

And when you run it, you'll get the instance ID (which you will need for this next part):

```
[ec2.Instance(id='i-02d42ec52027baa08')]
```

Figure 4.5 – EC2 instance created with a unique ID

You'll see that the instance with that same instance size and ID has been created on the AWS EC2 console:

Figure 4.6 – Running EC2 instance

2. Now, vertical scaling acts on that same instance but the instance size cannot be changed while it is running, so we will stop the instance first:

```python
import boto3

def stop_ec2():
    ec2_client = boto3.client("ec2")
    print(ec2_client.stop_instances(InstanceIds=["i-02d42ec52027baa08"]))

if __name__ == "__main__":
    stop_ec2()
```

Figure 4.7 – Function to stop an EC2 instance

This code will stop the instance when it is run. Confirm that the instance is stopped and note the size of the instance is still **t2.nano**:

☐	–	i-02d42ec52027baa08	⊖ Stopped	⊕ ⊖	t2.nano

Figure 4.8 – Stopped EC2 instance

3. Now, let's write the code to modify the instance into a `t2.micro` instance:

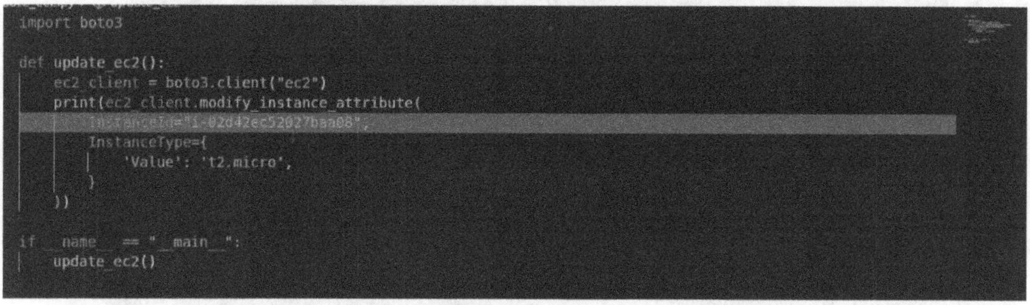

```python
import boto3

def update_ec2():
    ec2_client = boto3.client("ec2")
    print(ec2_client.modify_instance_attribute(
        InstanceId="i-02d42ec52027baa08",
        InstanceType={
            'Value': 't2.micro',
        }
    ))

if __name__ == "__main__":
    update_ec2()
```

Figure 4.9 – Code to update an EC2 instance

After running this code, you'll notice that on the console, your instance is now a **t2.micro** instance:

☐	–	i-02d42ec52027baa08	⊖ Stopped	⊕ ⊖	t2.micro

Figure 4.10 – Updated EC2 instance size

4. So, once you restart the instance, it will have that extra power available.

You may have noticed that this is a slog. And vertical scaling is – more often than not – a slog of downtime. While there are use cases for things like these (especially when you need to work with bigger individual machines), it's not the norm. Usually, horizontal autoscaling is better for your use case because of the lesser amount of downtime associated with the process. We'll dive into that now.

Autoscaling with Python based on a trigger

Autoscaling requires automating the process of increasing the available compute resources according to some sort of metric or statistic. In order to autoscale, we need to design a mechanism that will trigger our SDK call once a certain metric or threshold has been reached.

Understand that looking at this particular example from a singular cloud perspective may make it seem a little impractical because most cloud platforms have in-built autoscaling. The key here lies in fine-tuning that autoscaling. I'm going to create an **autoscaling group** and define the thresholds for scaling using a Python script. Then, I'm going to modify those thresholds and I will tell you the significance of why after I have done it.

Let's write a basic script to make an autoscaling group and put a threshold on it using a policy for CPU utilization. We'll go step-by-step from the launch configuration to the autoscaling group to the rule by which the instances will autoscale:

1. First, we write the code to create a launch configuration that all machines in the autoscaling group will follow:

```
#create a launch configuration for use in autoscaling
autoscaling.create_launch_configuration(
    LaunchConfigurationName="book_configuration",
    ImageId="ami-051f7e7f6c2f40dc1",
    InstanceType="t2.micro",
)
```

Figure 4.11 – Code to create a launch configuration

2. Next, we create the autoscaling group, which uses the launch configuration that we created previously:

```
#create an autoscaling group with your launch configuration
autoscaling.create_auto_scaling_group(
    AutoScalingGroupName="book_autoscaler",
    LaunchConfigurationName="book_configuration",
    MinSize=2,
    MaxSize=5,
    DesiredCapacity=2,
    AvailabilityZones=['us-east-1a', 'us-east-1b'],
)
```

Figure 4.12 – Code to create an autoscaling group

3. Finally, we will create a policy that will scale the group upward if CPU utilization is greater than 70%:

```
#create a policy for your autoscaling group
autoscaling.put_scaling_policy(
    AutoScalingGroupName="book_autoscaler",
    PolicyName="book_scale",
    PolicyType='TargetTrackingScaling',
    TargetTrackingConfiguration={
        'PredefinedMetricSpecification': {
            'PredefinedMetricType': 'ASGAverageCPUUtilization'
        },
        'TargetValue': 70
    }
)
```

Figure 4.13 – Code to create a scaling policy

Running all of these will give you a basic autoscaling group of virtual machines with these specifications. Now, you may be asking yourself where Python helps with this autoscaling. Well, for that, you first have to look at the metrics produced by these virtual machines.

If you look through the metrics that are produced by the VMs, you'll be able to find their CPU utilization metrics, which can be exported. Using these metrics, you can calculate the average utilization of CPUs over a period of time (that programming language Python helps, I'm told), then use that data to find a better autoscaling target. To modify the target, you can simply use the same code as before with a different metric value:

```
#update policy to 80 percent
autoscaling.put_scaling_policy(
    AutoScalingGroupName="book_autoscaler",
    (function) PolicyType: Any
    PolicyType='TargetTrackingScaling',
    TargetTrackingConfiguration={
        'PredefinedMetricSpecification': {
            'PredefinedMetricType': 'ASGAverageCPUUtilization'
        },
        'TargetValue': 80
    }
)
```

Figure 4.14 – Code for modified scaling policy

Your findings on the data may even reveal that there is a better metric to use for your workload than CPU utilization. You can modify that here as well.

This type of scaling is very useful and there are a lot of situations where you definitely will use these. However, this isn't the only way to implement scaling and virtualization. In the next section, we will explore containers and their roles and purpose in the field of scaling and virtualization.

Containers and where Python fits in with containers

Containers are small packages of software that serve as a unique runtime containing all of the necessary resources to run a small facet of an application, or sometimes the entire application itself.

The containers themselves are written in Go, as is the container orchestration service, Kubernetes. Those parts do not require Python unless the application code itself is written in Python. Where Python comes in handy is as the glue between the various containerized services. Orchestrating the orchestration, if you will.

Now, we are going to learn about the role that Python plays in the overall container picture. Python, as always, has a lot of libraries that support the use of containers and Kubernetes, and we will explore some of these libraries and how using Python can simplify your DevOps work where these important infrastructure elements are concerned.

Simplifying Docker administration with Python

Keeping Docker images together and organized is tricky. It's why they invented Kubernetes. But Kubernetes itself is tricky. This leaves two gaps:

- First, when there are multiple Docker images but complete orchestration with Kubernetes is not required
- Second, when Kubernetes APIs need to be frequently called or the cluster needs to be frequently updated

For both of these purposes, Python can be a useful tool. Remember this is about support, not refactoring. We're the auxiliary player here.

So, in this section, we will look at an example of how to use Python to administer multiple containers.

We will write a script to get a specific Docker image and create a container for it. This script can be rerun to do the same thing over and over again. You may also use the `restart` command if a container malfunctions. Now let's look at the code to pull Docker images and start a container:

```python
import docker

def docker_sample():
    client = docker.from_env()

    # Define the image name and tag
    image_name = 'python:latest'

    # Pull the image
    client.images.pull(image_name)

    # Create and run a container based on the pulled image
    container = client.containers.create(image_name)
    container.start()
    print(client.containers.list())

if __name__ == "__main__":
    docker_sample()
```

Figure 4.15 – Code to pull Docker images and start a container

It's simple, but that's the key to it. Its simplicity provides building blocks to improve upon.

But even if we keep it simple, sometimes the use of containers gets complex, which is where Kubernetes comes in. With Kubernetes comes its own challenges. These challenges can also be simplified and managed using Python.

Managing Kubernetes with Python

There will come a time in your container usage when Kubernetes will be the way that you need to go. At this time, Python can help as well. Python can help simplify a lot of Kubernetes administration tasks and since most Kubernetes workloads are run on the cloud, those SDKs are going to come in pretty handy as well.

I'm only going to include one example, which will consist of the manipulation of Kubernetes namespaces. Just to be safe, we don't want to crash and burn with computing resources yet, especially if you are new to Kubernetes.

Namespaces are abstractions within a Kubernetes cluster that are used to divide computer resources based on certain criteria. A criterion can be environment (dev, production, etc.), network restrictions, or based on resource quotas available to a namespace.

You can use Python to create and modify namespaces and manipulate the resources within them. Let's look at the steps to initialize a Kubernetes cluster and manage it using Python:

1. First, you will need to install Kubernetes with `pip` using the following command:

   ```
   pip install kubernetes
   ```

2. Next, let's write a script to create a few namespaces in our cluster. We can add resources to these namespaces later:

```python
from kubernetes import client, config

# Load Kubernetes configurations
config.load_kube_config()

# Create a Kubernetes client
api = client.CoreV1Api()

# Define namespaces
namespaces = ['ns1', 'ns2']
                        (variable) namespaces: list[str]
# Create namespac
for namespace in namespaces:
    namespace_client = client.V1Namespace(metadata=client.V1ObjectMeta(name=namespace))
    api.create_namespace(namespace_client)
```

Figure 4.16 – Code to create Kubernetes namespaces from a list

3. Now, let's write a policy for these namespaces and implement them into Kubernetes:

```
for namespace in namespaces:
    # Define the Network Policy manifest
    network_policy_manifest = {
        "apiVersion": "networking.k8s.io/v1",
        "kind": "NetworkPolicy",
        "metadata": {
            "name": "block-external-traffic",
            "namespace": namespace
        },
        "spec": {
            "podSelector": {},
            "policyTypes": ["Ingress"]
        }
    }

    # Create the Network Policy
    networking_api.create_namespaced_network_policy(namespace=namespace,
                                                    body=network_policy_manifest)
```

Figure 4.17 – Creating a policy for namespaces for implementation

This will create policies for both namespaces, which will block external traffic from outside the namespace. As you can see here, we've implemented the same formatted policy to both namespaces using an iterator. This is but one of the ways you can automate in Kubernetes using Python.

Eventually, you can automate these steps to the point where it will be possible for you to simply list out and visualize your Kubernetes cluster and press a couple of buttons to adjust it to your needs. Everything else, the cluster will take care of.

Summary

This chapter sent us on quite a trip in terms of how we use Python. We figured out how SDKs work, what advantages they have, and why Python is so useful to have in the world of SDK use. You can literally build applications on top of applications, I've seen it.

We also learned about scaling and how much of a hassle that is because of the balance you have to strike between availability and cost. Here, we also found use for Python and its great SDKs and data processing abilities, helping us strike that balance.

Containers are also greatly supported by Python libraries, which can help act as a glue filler in the gaps between Docker and Kubernetes. We learned about the assisting role that Python plays in the management of these services.

So, in conclusion, in this chapter you have learned quite a bit about Python's SDKs, using them for autoscaling, rightsizing, and containers. In the next chapter, we will take a closer look at how Python can be used to manipulate and interact with already provisioned resources.

Part 2: Sample Implementations of Python in DevOps

This part will cover sample implementations for some common DevOps use cases using Python.

This part has the following chapters:

- *Chapter 5, Manipulating Resources*
- *Chapter 6, Security and DevSecOps with Python*
- *Chapter 7, Automating Tasks*
- *Chapter 8, Understanding Event-Driven Architecture*
- *Chapter 9, Using Python for CI/CD Pipelines*

5
Manipulating Resources

*And into this Ring he poured his cruelty, his malice, and his will to dominate all
life. One Ring to rule them all.*

– Galadriel (Lord of the Rings)

In the previous chapter, we talked about creating resources. We talked about using automation to provision the correct specifications of resources every single time. But what about pre-existing resources?

In some real-world scenarios, you may be expected to work with projects or workloads that you haven't created from scratch, or that need to be touched with a very fine hand. You may also be working with resources that you have a lot less power over, such as managed resources in your cloud that are managed by your cloud provider.

It's easy to manipulate the resources that you have made, but these legacy resources and resources that have fewer controls are the challenge for **DevOps** engineers. Conquering these challenges requires learning how to manipulate resources to make them more inclined to the DevOps philosophy. Whether that involves a change in approach in the resources, the code, the architecting process, or just understanding the workload better, we can use the philosophy of DevOps to make resources better provisioned and better performing.

Speaking of performance, one of the best indicators of how future performance should look is past performance. If the usage of resources can give us a pattern, we can use this pattern to predict the provisioning of resources better and streamline our workload. Besides that, any insight that we gain regarding not just usage patterns but how the DevOps team and the application team handle the resources and react to events is useful for future reference.

Being predictive in the approaches that you take can be very useful, but these predictions must always be made on the back of solid data. If we are to predict and adapt, it must be done according to some sort of logic. This logic must be understood (there are people in this world who do things just because they're told how to do it one way; they're useful but they cannot adapt) fully to allow for effective action to be taken.

The primary goal of this chapter is to help you learn how to look at the resources you have and to use them to maximum effect. This means understanding how the resources scale up and down, as well as the history and historical components of those resources.

With that, in this chapter, we will cover the following topics:

- Modifying resources to adjust to demand using Python as a trigger for events
- Analyzing live and historical data and using it for future workloads
- Refactoring a legacy application slowly over time

Technical requirements

To complete this chapter, you will require the following:

- A GitHub account
- Python
- An AWS account

Event-based resource adjustment

Resources are money. Literally. In the world of DevOps, the norm is that the more resources you use, the more money that you spend. That's simple enough, right? But the problem comes when the return from those resources is not enough to cover their costs. One of the main reasons this happens is because the resources that are consumed are done so at a constant rate, even if they are not required. For optimal resource consumption, a new method was created one with which resources are only consumed at the time of their use and are then downsized appropriately until their next use. Let's say that you are on a shopping spree. You don't know exactly how much you're going to spend, you have only a vague idea of how much you are going to spend on the items. You are probably going to go over the tentative budget that you have set for yourself and in addition to that, you might not even be happy with everything that you bought.

DevOps is a lot like that – it is about the groceries (resources), how much you spend on them, and how much value you can get out of them. One of the most common ways to keep track of a grocery/ expenses budget is to make a nice spreadsheet where you can tally up everything. Here, again, there are similarities to DevOps, though in DevOps, you are usually given an exact quote by your resource provider and it's easier to find better deals than with groceries – trust me.

Now, for the final part of the grocery section, you adjust the groceries you buy according to the events that you have, right? If your friend's vegan, you cook vegan stuff. If they have diabetes, sugar is off the menu. If you're by yourself, you can buy a tub of ice cream with no judgment. That's exactly what we want with our event-based adjustments. You can use the type of event that is being brought to you to adjust the resources being provided. You can look at the events that are going on and adapt your resources accordingly.

We are going to show this concept while considering a couple of examples – one that deals with the global distribution of localized content and another that deals with testing a new feature for a website on a small subset of users.

Edge location-based resource sharing

One of the most difficult challenges that we have with a global application is load time for resources. If a user is too far from the closest data center, it can result in a significant amount of lag and latency when they use their application. For this reason, most companies with applications on a major scale have data centers and edge caches in high-population areas/areas with high web traffic. An **edge** or **edge location** is just a data center that is closer to the target user, making their load time faster. **Edge caches** are user and website data (such as cookies) stored in edge locations for faster access for that user. This helps users get to data centers that can serve them the fastest.

However, the question now becomes, how do we direct these users to the appropriate data centers or caches that will give them the lowest latency? To do that, we must find a way to acquire the location data for the user's device and reference that data to redirect that user to the closest data center.

To do this, we can write a function that takes a web traffic request and extracts certain headers from it. Let's look at the code for this:

```
''' the request variable is a json that contains the request headers
and body'''
def process_request(request):
'''get all headers'''
headers  = request["headers"]
''' we're using country in this example, but this is any arbitrary
header you  choose to pass '''
request_country = headers["country"]
''' throw to a function that maps each available server to a country
'''
server = server_map(request_country)
''' return value from correct server as prescribed by server map '''
return server_response(server, request)
```

What this code does is pick out the country header, which you will need to define yourself (which is good, because you can customize it), and then direct the web request to the appropriate server. A small layer in between the request and response can work wonders for connectivity. You can see an illustration of this in the subsequent figure:

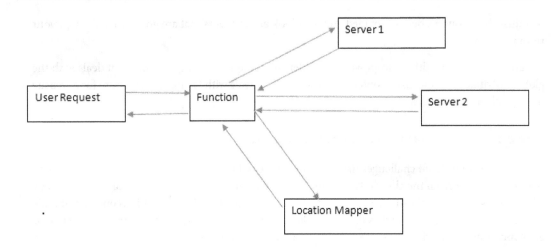

Figure 5.1 – Function to facilitate location mapping for servers

Now that we have learned how to redirect users to custom locations, let's look at how to redirect features toward a custom set of users.

Testing features on a subset of users

When an application needs to implement a new feature and the application team wants that feature to be tested in a live environment, the need arises for some sort of mechanism that sorts a small subset of users into a group that will receive that new feature. The analytical data acquired from this group will then be used to judge the feature and its effectiveness based on certain criteria. The reverse – removal of a feature – works this way as well. If you recall when YouTube removed the numbers from their dislike button, some users still had their numbers for weeks because of their cached website versions. Even after that, browser extensions came out that extracted the dislike number from the YouTube API itself for whichever video you were watching (that is, until YouTube took it out of their API entirely).

Now, you may be wondering why such a test would be necessary given the fact that the feature had probably been tested over and over again, even before it had been launched. Well, here's the thing:

- **It might not have been**: You'll be surprised how many companies are willing to put a new thing out there for a small subset to use without going through user acceptance testing. You'll be even more surprised to learn that this isn't a bad strategy sometimes (but if you are going to do this, I suggest you do it with the example I'm going to give you in the upcoming code block).

- **Users break stuff**: It is the nature of users to break stuff in ways that testers cannot comprehend. You cannot fully understand human nature and the chaos behind it and any invention you make must be tested against it. Having a more controlled approach requires throwing your work to a subsample of chaos and hoping that it can endure.

This method of testing is commonly referred to as the **A/B testing method**.

Now that that's out of the way, we can get to the implementation. This implementation is very similar to that of the implementation for the edge locations and involves a proxy very much in that vein.

We're going to subset our users in two ways: randomly and based on some criteria. First, let's look at the code for the random distribution of user requests (20% to one server and 80% to the other server):

```
''' get request from user '''
def process_request(request):
''' get a random number between 1 and 10 '''
num = random.randrange(1,10)
''' conditionally return site containing special feature '''
if num<=2:
return special_response(request)
else:
return regular_response(request)
```

You can choose a less arbitrary range if you'd like. Just remember to track the statistics between these two responses differently to get the correct insights. An alternative to this is **feature flags**, but that requires dividing users into subsets based on certain criteria, which is what we are about to cover in the following code block. The preceding method is good if you don't want to distinguish between users or can't and just want activity data:

```
''' get request from user '''
def process_request(request):
'''get request header with feature flag '''
header = request["header"]
feature = header["feature"]
''' Check if feature flag is turned on, i.e. if it is True or False
'''
if feature:
return featured_response(request)
else:
return normal_response(request)
```

Here, we can see the users who have feature flags getting the featured response (the unique response they get if their feature flag is on). These featured responses are different from the regular responses. The activation of the feature flag can be a random edit made to the database or an opt-in offer given to the user. Once again, the data for these two resources needs to be distinguished for maximum effectiveness.

Speaking of data (and I have been), now that we have all of this analytical and operational data from people using the feature flags and those who are not, as well as the occurrence of all of these events, we must do something with it – we need to analyze it and generate insights.

Analyzing data

I have found that – as an adult – I have increasingly become more and more responsible for myself. However, this responsibility and the person that I am right now have come from a series of events in my past. Mistakes, successes, and everything in between have defined me and my approach to life.

A lot of my approaches to life also happen to be approaches to DevOps – that's just how that panned out. Through the life (and DevOps) lessons that I have learned, I've found two things: you must live for the person you are right now, and that person is defined by your past and yet is not the same person as in the past.

Your workload follows a similar pattern. It is based on your history but cannot completely be considered the same as it was previously. The code has probably changed, the infrastructure is different, and even the personnel that implement it most likely have changed. However, with all that being said, there are still lessons to be learned from the past. Important lessons.

Earlier in this book (*Chapter 1, Introducing DevOps Principles,* to be exact), I emphasized the need for **monitoring** and **logging**, and I said that these were great tools for event handling and maintaining the historical performance of your workload. Now, we will begin exploring how that historical performance can give us insights that we can use to our advantage.

We will look at a couple of analysis techniques: analysis of **live data** and analysis of **historical data**. Each presents challenges. Each can act as a template to solve a fairly common DevOps problem.

Analysis of live data

Live or streaming data is data that is constantly being processed by a system at present. It is data that's being received or returned by a system. A system lives off of the data that it absorbs and generates (*input -> process -> output*). The system is shaped by this data and sometimes, in the case of critical systems, it needs to be molded by this data. To make tactical decisions based on recent data, collecting live data and immediate insights on that data is necessary.

Most clouds and monitoring systems come with default ways to store and analyze live data. And for the most part, they are quite effective. They can store data and generate insights on that data to a certain extent. However, sometimes, a custom approach is necessary. And this is where Python excels. Not because of speed, but because of convenience and a pre-built library for analysis, Python (even with only its default libraries) can perform data analysis and conversion on practically any kind of data that a system gives out.

So, let's look at an example where we use Python's built-in **marshal library** to decode a **byte string**:

```
import marshal
''' function to decode bytes '''
def decode_bytes(data):
''' Load binary data into readable data with marshal '''
```

```
result = marshal.loads(data)
''' Return raw data '''
return result
```

Byte strings are often used in **network communication** and **cryptography** (both of which usually involve live data), and converting them into other languages may require adding libraries and possibly creating custom data types. There's no such need with Python.

But this usually accounts for smaller sizes of data and recent data, sometimes as recent as the last millisecond. For a truly historic analysis, you need millions of rows of data. You also need something that can analyze that data. Here, Python excels even more.

Analysis of historical data

Live data can help us make adjustments; they are tactical. But to be truly strategic – to think about the big picture and to think long term – you need historical data and a way to analyze it. The past contains a lot of data; this data contains patterns, and it is in these patterns that the key to optimizing your workload lies.

The analysis of historical data requires converting the data into a format where it can be mass-read by a program. Once this data has been formatted, it can be fed into an algorithm that processes the data into useful information that the data engineer may want.

Dealing with historical data usually means dealing with data that is consistent and high in volume. However, one of the potential variables can be whether the data is uniform or not. Oftentimes, when the software to record data is changed or upgraded, certain aspects of the data change as well. Reconciling the old and the new historical data is one of the challenges that DevOps engineers working with data can face.

The next challenge that the engineers potentially face is the ability to present the data in a format that either humans or machines can read. For humans, this would be some sort of document or visualization. For machines, this would be some data format that they can read.

Regardless, all of this data requires mass data analysis. You can achieve this even faster by using Python's **multiprocessing library** to batch-process a large amount of data in parallel by leveraging multiple CPU cores for this purpose. Let's dive into the process of using multiple CPU cores with code:

```
import multiprocessing
''' Get list and return sum '''
def get_sum(numerical_array):
''' return sum of array '''
return sum(numerical_array)
'''method that calls sum method to get total sum for 1 million records
'''
def get_total_sum(full_array):
```

```
''' Initialize 4 processors '''
pool = multiprocessing.Pool(processes=4)
''' List of sums in 10,000 number blocks '''
sum_list = []
''' Get 10,000 values at a time for sum out of 1,000,000''''
for i in range(0, count(full_array)/10000):
sum_array = full_array[i*10000:(i+1)*10000]
'''Make an array of 10,000 length arrays '''
sum_list.append(sum_array)
''' Get final array of sums of  each 10,000 value array '''
final_array_list = pool.map(get_sum, sum_list)
''' Get one final sum of all these elements '''
return sum(final_array_list)
```

So, in this code, an array of 1 million values is divided into 100 arrays of 10,000 values, each of which is summed up to calculate the total for their array. This is done on one of four different processors at the same time using the multiprocessing library. Breaking down this large task into smaller tasks can optimally use resources for data processing.

Well, all of this is nice enough. But where does the data come from? Usually, your applications. Well, for the data to be good, the application has to be good, right? Yes, but that is not always the case. Let's look at what happens when some applications remain stagnant and become stale.

Refactoring legacy applications

A clean slate is one of the most convenient things in the world. I am going to show you two sheets of paper, and you can tell me which one you'd want to draw on:

Figure 5.2 – A new application versus a legacy application, illustrated

If you chose the right one, congratulations – you are now a DevOps engineer! Don't look too deeply into this particular drawing; it's just some rubbish I put together.

You see, DevOps engineers rarely get to work with their code. Even developers getting to work with their code is getting rarer these days. In my experience, I have only worked with a clean slate on a project in any non-personal capacity once or twice. Many of you who are just starting may have only worked with either projects you coded yourself or little template projects you may have found. However, in a real-life scenario, that is quite rare.

Even if you work with a blank slate, unless you have built assembly code with your own customized operating system, there are still a lot of dependencies that your workload relies on (and if you are doing it this way, how bored are you?).

99% of what you work with is built with something somebody else worked on – sometimes, hundreds and thousands of somebodies with varying levels of skill, competencies, and opinions. You walk a path built by a multitude of architects (and sometimes with no roadmaps/documentation).

You see, initially, it's simple – you start with the latest version of the code, you host it on `localhost`, and voila, you are the master of your world. But then, you realize that everyone did this and everyone is desperate to hold onto that sense of control, even in a professional environment, regardless of the consequences upon the quality of their work. That is how you end up with critical infrastructure that hasn't been updated in 5 years, critical services that run on discontinued products, and a team that is unwilling *and* unable (not either, both) to change it for the better. That is how you end up with tech debt (technical slang for horrible planning skills).

To get out of technical debt, you have three options: optimize, refactor, or restart. What that means is you have three choices (not just in DevOps, but in life too): live with your mistakes, improve upon them, or start fresh. What you want to do (and what you can do) depends on both you and your circumstances. We will look at all three of these options so that you can figure out which one is best for your workload.

Optimize

Your first option is **optimization**. You can look at what you have right now and make sure that it runs optimally, consuming the optimum amount of resources while being available to the user with all of its functions intact. A lot of the time (especially in **Site Reliability Engineering** (SRE), a field where you work in practically nothing but legacy applications) optimizing your legacy application might be your only option if you're working with a critical application that cannot change one aspect without having to change many others – a monolith, if you will. These limitations are why a lot of companies look to break out of the monolith.

In the case of optimizing legacy applications, we are very limited in what we can do. But that doesn't mean we can't do anything. One of the most important DevOps concepts is **Desired State Configuration** (**DSC**) and the reason for that is maintaining systems such as these.

In a DSC, the virtual machine is given certain configurations that it must maintain. The state of these configurations is checked from time to time. If the state has changed significantly, then it is reset and brought back to the original desired state.

This all happens behind the scenes and doesn't truly affect the application. It is probably the best way to handle an application that cannot be refactored or containerized into Docker containers.

Refactor

If you're working with anything resembling decent code or resembling a decent project team (big ifs, but bear with me), then you may only be working with a workload that is either outdated and needs an update plus adjustments or one that no longer fulfills all that is required of it. In these cases, there is a healthy middle ground between the old and the new in **refactoring**.

Refactoring your code base could involve simple things such as upgrading a dependency, writing a new component, or removing unnecessary components. It could also involve a long and arduous process such as separating a website's frontend and backend.

So, let's look at the most prominent method of refactoring that there is: the strangler fig. In nature, a strangler fig is a plant that uses a tree as a base to grow and eventually strangles the tree to death and replaces it. The strangler fig works similarly for legacy applications.

Here are the steps to perform strangler fig refactoring:

1. **Separate the database**: If the database server hasn't been separated from the application server, do so now. This will help the scalability of both.

2. **Turn third-party API calls into functions/microservices**: If any third-party APIs are being called that you do not directly maintain, separate them into function calls that can later be called by your refactored application. Separate them from the rest of the backend.

3. **Separate the backend and frontend**: Separate the backend parts that deal with the data and the frontend parts that deal with user interaction. These parts need to communicate with each other using a buffer known as a **frontend for backend**, which is a middleman for API interactions with the frontend.

4. **Separate non-critical backend functions into microservices**: Separate the services that only process data and do not interact with the database into smaller microservices that can then process data independently and with greater scale.

5. **Create a database connection mechanism and put the rest of the backend into microservices**: Finally, the heart of the application becomes loosely coupled thanks to **database connection strings**, which allow the data to be manipulated from anywhere given the correct credentials.

That sounds a bit tricky, doesn't it? Well, it is. But it's also rewarding... sometimes. Refactoring an application – regardless of effectiveness – is one of the most effective ways you can practically learn about making an application and maintaining it. But it is quite a drain on the mind. Don't you wish you could just get away from all of these mistakes other people before you made and start with a clean slate? Well, if you do, then the next section will fit in great with your plans.

Restart

Sometimes – and I hope for your sake that that time is early in the development process – you need to throw the things you have out entirely and start fresh. A blank slate, as I have stated before, is the easiest starting point. If you believe that your application is beyond saving and that no insight or use can be salvaged from it, then you can build your application from scratch.

A lot of the time, it doesn't make sense to migrate components between old and new applications either because of stack incompatibility or because the old components offer nothing of value. In these cases, the most valuable thing is the data generated by the old application and migrating that data to a database that can interact with the new application.

If you're making a new application, honestly, do it your way. But here's some advice:

- Make decisions that are long term and not just based on what you're thinking about now.

- Make decisions that put quality first, but also understand that mistakes will always be there.

- Don't react to everything; being reactive will 100% result in a worse application. If you can help it, don't react to anything. Be proactive.

- Put quality, readability, and maintainability first. Don't think that you'll come back to something later. That kind of thinking adds many hours of work on your shoulders (or even worse, somebody else's) later.

Restarting an application and building it from scratch is an appealing concept. Don't restart too much, though, because you'll never get anything done. There are only so many times you can restart a project before you realize that maybe your approach is the problem.

Summary

This chapter took a few detours that you may have not seen coming. It was a chapter about simplicity, finding better ways to get your work done, and optimizing the use of your resources to get that work done.

You learned how to deliver content to your users faster and in a more customized way while at the same time collecting their data for analytical insights. You also learned the methods and formats of this data collection process, as well as the important role that Python can play in processing this data.

You also learned about applications, how most application waste is created, and how this can bog down your workload and your successors for years to come. You also learned a few ways to either mitigate, get around, or eliminate this problem.

So, in conclusion, you have now figured out that manipulating resources is about being efficient not just for the resources, but for the sake of your own time. I hope that you reflect on this chapter for your DevOps workloads and your grocery shopping.

In the next chapter, we are going to cover a particularly favorite topic of mine: automation. We are going to find ways we can make our lives easier and less bothered by things we shouldn't be bothered with.

6

Security and DevSecOps with Python

It's a jungle out there. Disorder and confusion everywhere...

– Randy Newman

(If you know the rest of the song, good for you.)

What is the password that you use most frequently? Do you never re-use a password? Don't lie to me and don't lie to yourself in this situation, lest you get locked out of your accounts. I'm using passwords here because that is the easiest way to break the ice on this conversation about security, and passwords are the easiest way to think about security. They provide a secure way to distinguish accounts and users and allow each their own access parameters. What we are going to talk about in this chapter will be a little more complex (just a little) but the underlying principles are the same: it is about securing access and making sure only the right people have access.

In **DevSecOps** (a branch of **DevOps** dedicated to security), the goal is to have security measures present and used before, during, and after any breach in security. This requires the use of best practices in securing access keys and other credentials, the use of best practices in securing infrastructure (such as containers), and the same for after a security incident has occurred.

Security is the responsibility of every single person on an application's team and this responsibility obligates the team members to use tools and techniques that do not compromise on security and that can facilitate the automation of security processes to remove human error.

It just so happens we know a very good facilitator for that, don't we? That's right, **Python** is incredible at facilitating and supporting security and encryption and it is flexible and easy enough to use for security engineers even if they don't have a lot of coding experience. Python's Swiss Army knife property gives it the ability to integrate anywhere within this chapter.

So, let's view the content that we are going to explore in this chapter:

- We will find out how to secure and obfuscate sensitive codes, API keys, and passwords using Python
- We will learn what validation of containers is and how Python can help double-check this process if needed
- We will learn about the tools that Python has that can be used to facilitate incident monitoring and response

Technical requirements

Here are some requirements that will help you follow along with this chapter's activities:

- A GitHub account to clone the repository containing sample code
- An AWS account
- A Google Cloud account
- Google Colab
- Any environment with Python installed
- Tolerance for my sarcastic prose

You can access this book's repository at `https://github.com/PacktPublishing/Hands-On-Python-for-DevOps`

Securing API keys and passwords

API keys and passwords are valuable for the reason most things are valuable: they cost money and the data protected by them are valuable. If you've ever watched any heist movie (and if you haven't, I'd recommend *Heat*, which is a great movie) you know that there is always some sort of access code, signature, or safe combination that the heist team must acquire. This is because the idea of a secret code, passphrase, or encryption is perpetual throughout human civilization as a barrier to accessing sensitive information. Passwords existed for tens of thousands of years before computers even came around.

A heist team in the cyber domain will also try a similar strategy. They will attempt to extract passcodes and credentials from people who potentially have them so that they can acquire sensitive information. Sometimes, the information inside doesn't even have to be sensitive, sometimes people just hack things because they are bored or like to social engineer people (I'm told there are people addicted to manipulating people, so that is quite scary). Either way, your information security is under constant attack, whether it is on the server side or the user side. So, precautionary measures and mechanisms for these kinds of attacks are necessary.

Now, we get to the Python part. We can try a couple of things with Python to implement this concept here. We can create environment variables and secrets that store variables that are sensitive in a separate folder or within the **operating system (OS)** configuration itself. We can also use Python (by itself or with some other tool or API) to extract and obfuscate **personally identifiable information (PII)**.

Store environment variables

Environment variables are stored as both a means of separating credentials from application code to prevent hardcoding and to make sure that an application can run with different credentials on different systems just by configuring those credentials into the OS or a file.

That brings us to the two ways in which we can store and retrieve environment variables: we can store them as files or as variables defined in the OS. You can, of course, also do this in a Cloud Secret Manager or using a hardware device, but those are similar concepts to the ones we are discussing.

For the first way (files), you can create and read from .env files in the following way:

1. These files are the standard for storing these environment variables and are usually ignored in practically every .gitignore file. To read these files, we must first install Python's python-dotenv library:

    ```
    pip install python-dotenv
    ```

2. After this, we can create a .env file and store variables and secrets within it. We separate these secrets based on the line that they are on. Here is a sample of a couple of lines of a .env file:

    ```
    API_KEY = <insert_key_here>
    API_SECRET_KEY = <insert_secret_key_here>
    ```

    Remember, *all caps* are for constants. This approach helps consolidate these constants in one place so that you don't have to worry about changing them in all the locations you need them in your code, and you don't have to worry about missing one change somewhere.

3. Now, let's write the code by which our program can access the environment variables:

    ```
    from dotenv import load_dotenv
    import os

    #load .env file
    load_dotenv()

    #load API keys into variables
    api_key = os.getenv("API_KEY")
    api_secret_key = os.getenv("API_SECRET_KEY")
    ```

Running this code will give you the API key and the secret key in their respective variables.

Next, let's try the same thing, but with environment variables exported and used directly from our own OS:

1. In Linux – where most servers of this kind are prevalent – we can set up environment variables as we did in the previous example with the following commands:

    ```
    export API_KEY = <insert_key_here>
    export API_SECRET_KEY = <insert_secret_key_here>
    ```

    These will set the environment variables having the names API_KEY and API_SECRET_KEY in your OS.

2. Now comes the matter of accessing these values:

    ```
    import os

    # Get the API key and secret access key from the environment
    api_key = os.environ.get("API_KEY")
    api_secret_key = os.environ.get("API_SECRET_KEY")
    ```

    You'll see that we are still using the os library from the previous code. This method is a little bit simpler and perhaps a little more secure than the .env file for a fewer number of environment variables. But when using a large number of environment variables, a .env file is better at aggregation and easier to use and handle.

These methods have taught you how to deal with sensitive information that you are responsible for and you yourself add to the code base. However, there comes a time when you will have to deal with the sensitive data of others. This data needs to be protected and you need to ensure that it doesn't get into the wrong hands. The key to this? Making it useless for anything other than your purposes. We will talk about the obfuscation of PII next.

Extract and obfuscate PII

A person's sensitive personal information is one of the most valuable things they have: financially, socially, and intimately. Compromising the security of this information can result in great harm to the person in all three of these areas. The privacy of people is of utmost importance, and we must take all possible measures in order to preserve it, especially when they entrust some bit of that information to the services that we provide for them.

So, what would be the best approach to start with this? Well, there are a lot of pre-built services such as Amazon Macie or Google Cloud's **DLP** (short for **Data Loss Prevention**), and these services are handy, but you may not understand the inner workings of them since they are trained on certain machine learning algorithms that require very little input (if at all) from their users to redact and obfuscate a wide range of personal information.

But let's say there is a piece of information that isn't covered by these services, or you cannot use them because of compliance reasons. Then, you would have to begin creating your solution from scratch. Here again, Python is your friend. You can use Python to read files and find locations that contain sensitive information (based on certain criteria) and change that information in a way that hides or obfuscates it. This technique is the same as that for mining data by finding important patterns within the data, only in this case, instead of extracting the data, we are making sure that if some malicious actors tried to extract it, they would not be able to recover any vital information.

To demonstrate this, we are going to use a very simple **regex** or **regular expression** pattern for phone numbers to find them within a text and replace them with some form of redaction. We could try something a bit more complex, but it would still be the same concept, and if you are new to regex, I would suggest that you start somewhat slowly and discover the magic of regex. Truly, you will feel like a wizard.

Enough posturing for now; let's get down to business. First, we need a regex that can be used to capture the pattern of a phone number. Don't try and make a regex yourself unless you're really trying to dive deep into it. For most use cases, you can find a suitable regex pre-made for you on the internet. In most cases, you can use it as it is, and in some very specific cases, you might have to make a couple of adjustments. So, the regex that covers phone number patterns (both using country codes and not) can be written like this: \d{3}-\d{3}-\d{4}'.

That probably looks like a bunch of gibberish to you, but it works, and you should trust that (someone probably lost their mind trying to get it just right). This works with dashes and without country codes (though, you can make a regex that works with both). Now, let's implement the regex on a small passage that contains phone numbers:

```python
#initial text
import re
text = "The first number is 901-895-7906. The second number is: 081-
548-3262"

#pattern for search
search_pattern = r'\d{3}-\d{3}-\d{4}'

#replacement for pattern
replacement_text = "<phone_number>"

#text replacement
new_text = re.sub(search_pattern, replacement_text, text)

#output given: "The first number is <phone_number>. The second number
is: <phone_number>"
print(new_text)
```

Well, there you have it; this code finds phone numbers using a regex pattern and subsequently obfuscates it by replacing the phone numbers.

This is by far one of the simplest and most accessible ways to get regex but you can get even more complex with it. You can use it to obfuscate social security numbers, passport numbers, and pretty much anything that matches a pre-defined pattern.

So far, we have had security on the simplest, textual level. Now, we need to look towards security for our infrastructure. For this, we can look at container images since they are so prevalent, and validating them is so important. Let's see how we can validate these images.

Validating and verifying container images with Binary Authorization

The amount of time I have now spent harping on about containers has probably clued you into the fact that containers may be somewhat important. Containers are, of course, an encapsulation of all the resource requirements and libraries that are specifically needed to run one service in an application. Containers being isolated from each other results in the elimination of conflict between the libraries required to run the services in each container, effectively creating an isolated system for each service in an overall large system or application.

However, this also presents a two-fold vulnerability: complexity and a larger threat vector in some circumstances. Handling all of these containers and the complex underlying libraries that lie within them (thus the need for Kubernetes) can be a difficult task. Managing these complex systems improperly can lead to the creation of structural and informational vulnerabilities in the system. At the same time, if multiple clusters are exposed to a public-facing setting or can be accessed in some way that gives an unauthorized user privileged access to your system, the threat to one container could threaten all the containers present in your system, as well as all your information.

Python's Docker libraries make sure that you can do this for every layer of your image in an automated manner. Python can also use a number of third-party image verification tools. We will explore one of those tools with Google's Binary Authorization API and Workflow for Kubernetes. So, let's see how to verify compliant images with Binary Authorization!

Compliance is an interesting subject, much of it is in the eye of the beholder. The definition of compliance depends on how strict you want to be. In Kubernetes – specifically in **Google Kubernetes Engine** – there must be some sort of assurance or regulation that defines that the correct image has been used. The mechanic is known as **Binary Authorization**.

Binary Authorization allows the Docker containers that are deployed in a Kubernetes cluster to be checked according to certain criteria. Authorization can be done either by using a compliance policy or an attestor. A compliance policy creates rules that allow only images that meet a certain criterion. Adding an attestor means adding an individual user in your project who can testify that the image that is going to be used is correct. In Binary Authorization, you can use one or both of these in order to authorize your images for your Kubernetes cluster. Let's see how to do that:

1. We are now going to write a script to create an attestor and assign that attestor to the Kubernetes engine. First, we must install the client libraries for containers and Binary Authorization:

```
pip install google-cloud-binary-authorization google-cloud-
container
```

2. Now, let's write the script for the Binary Authorization of the cluster:

```
from google.cloud import binaryauthorization_v1

def sample_create_attestor():
    client = binaryauthorization_
v1.BinauthzManagementServiceV1Client()

    attestor = binaryauthorization_v1.Attestor()
    attestor.name = <Enter_attestor_name>

    request = binaryauthorization_v1.CreateAttestorRequest(
        parent=<Enter_parent_value_of_attestor>,
        attestor_id=<Enter_attestor_id>,
        attestor=attestor,
    )


    client.create_attestor(request=request)
```

This will create an attestor that can attest your cluster requests.

3. Now, we need to add the Binary Authorization to a cluster that has already been created or is about to be created:

```
from google.cloud import container_v1

def sample_update_cluster():
    client = container_v1.ClusterManagerClient()

    request = container_v1.UpdateClusterRequest(
"desired_node_pool_id": <Node_pool_to_update>,
"update": {
"desired_binary_authorization": {
"enabled": True,
```

```
"evaluation_mode": 2
    }
  }
)

client.update_cluster(request=request)
```

This script will update the Kubernetes cluster to start using our Binary Authorization method. That takes care of incidents within your infrastructure.

Now, we will explore a couple of things that could help you with incidents outside of your infrastructure.

Incident monitoring and response

How would one define an incident? Well, let me posit this to you: what would you do if a bear attacked you? Does this sound stupid? Are these way too many questions? Well, this question is a fairly direct way to understand an incident and how it is reacted to.

The bear is attacking you; it is much larger than you and, well, you don't want it to get you. In this case, the bear attack is the incident and the bear itself is just a vector for the incident. The result of the incident depends on the response, and to have a good response, you need a good head on your shoulders (you need to *monitor* the situation, get it?). The report of the response to the incident will happen one way or another. However, if you want to be the one writing the report, you need to have handled the incident correctly.

Actual security incidents are not as brutal as that (not physically, anyway). Don't worry. But they do work similarly. There is an incident, in which security is compromised in some way, there is a tool used to exploit a vulnerability, and when that vulnerability is exploited, it must be handled calmly and mitigated where possible. Once that is done and you have restored order, the incident response needs to be documented and distributed to the correct parties.

Now, here is where Python comes in. In order to respond to a security threat that potentially targets a fleet of virtual machines, Python can help run what is called a **runbook**, which is a series of commands that can be deployed to reset a system or to have it respond to some sort of threat. Another way to use Python in this capacity would be to look at monitoring data from the time of an incident and compare it to regular data in order to find some patterns that can be used to predict and get ahead of future incidents.

Running runbooks

When we talk about incident response, one of the most common responses to an incident that affects your resources is to turn it on and off again. This is effective maybe 97% of the time. Seriously. But sometimes people resent doing that, too. For me, when the Bluetooth malfunctions on my laptop,

I have to restart it for some reason. It's irrational and it irritates me irrationally, but it provides the solution (unlike the 500 other ways to restart Bluetooth that I find on the internet before I actually go through with it).

We're going to play it smart; we are going to focus on that 97%, but at the same time, we are going to give you the blueprint to run more complex code and procedures that you may like to write. This one is particularly closely adapted to AWS, but similar fleet management and operations can be found on every major cloud as well as for most on-premises operations as well.

For this exercise, we are using the **AWS EventBridge** to trigger a step function that will subsequently run a command on the desired EC2 instance that has triggered the event, restarting the instance from within. Again, we're keeping the commands simple here, but if you want you can get more advanced with it. So, let's get started:

1. Let's start with a running instance. I have named mine `test1`. Very creative, I know.

Figure 6.1 – A running instance

Let's live in a scenario where this is an instance that has a high amount of network traffic flowing through it. So high that, if it dropped below a certain level, it would indicate some sort of malfunction in the instance. In this case, that malfunction can be sorted through a simple restart using a runbook document.

2. Let's make the structure for that command now in **AWS Lambda**. But first, we need the command that is to be sent, which is found in **Systems Manager**. Open **Systems Manager** and go to the **Documents** tab at the bottom of the sidebar:

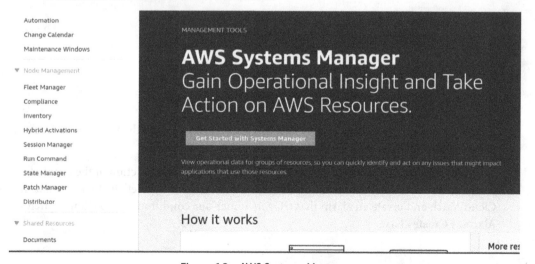

Figure 6.2 – AWS Systems Manager

3. Within the documents, search for the `AWS-RestartEC2Instance` document. This is the default document, and you can base a lot of other VM manipulation documents on it:

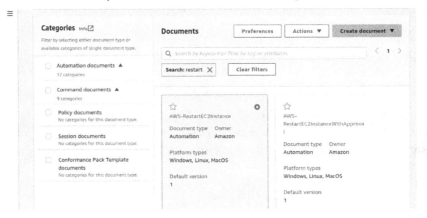

Figure 6.3 – Document to perform EC2 restarts

This is a simple baseline document and it can serve as a baseline for any sort of scripting action that you perform. Most other cloud providers also have something equivalent to this.

Figure 6.4 – Detailed AWS-RestartEC2Instance document

If we look at it a bit closer, we can see that this document stops and then starts a particular instance based on instance ID, which is what we are going to provide.

4. Now, let's write an EventBridge event that will trigger a Lambda function in the event of a decrease in network traffic over the course of five minutes. For that, let's first go to Amazon CloudWatch and create an alarm that triggers under our condition. Go to **CloudWatch** | **Alarms** | **Create alarm**.

Figure 6.5 – Cloudwatch Alarms console

We can now create a separate alarm for our `test 1` instance and it will be shown graphically to give you an idea of what is happening with the metric currently:

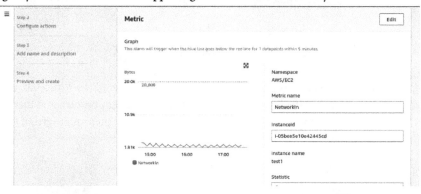

Figure 6.6 – Creating an alarm metric

5. Next, let's set the condition for the trigger for the alarm to be under **20,000** bytes of network input over a period of five minutes:

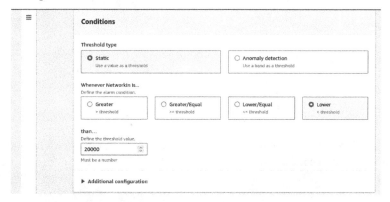

Figure 6.7 – Setting a threshold for the alarm

6.   Name the alarm `test1-alarm` in the field asking you for the alarm name and we're good to go.

Now, we can look at the alarm on the **Details** tab and find the EventBridge rules, which we will need to set up the EventBridge trigger:

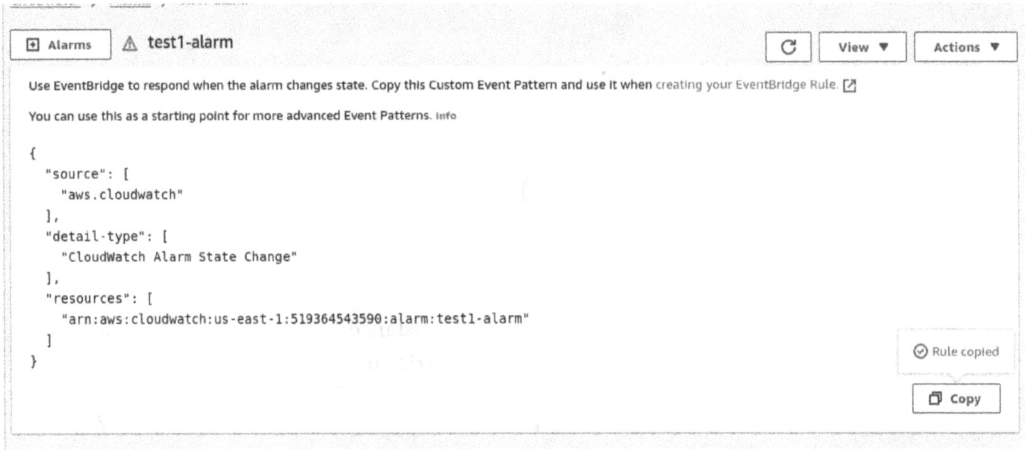

Figure 6.8 – Alarm configuration details

7.   Then, go to **Amazon EventBridge** in the AWS section, and then to the **Rules** tab, where you will create a new event. On the first page, select **Rule with an Event pattern** and then move on to the next page. Here, you will paste the EventBridge rule that you acquired from the alarm:

Figure 6.9 – Pattern creation for event bridge

8.   Now that you have the pattern, press **Next**, then in another tab, open AWS Lambda. Here, we will write our Python code to execute the restart of the EC2 instance.

In AWS Lambda, choose the Python execution time and maintain all of the default settings otherwise. Then, add the following code:

```
import json
import boto3


client = boto3.client('ssm')


def lambda_handler(event, context):

    instance_id = event["instanceids"]
    client.send_command(InstanceIds = [instance_id],
DocumentName = "AWS-RestartEC2Instance")
    return "Command to restart has been sent."
```

This code will send the command of the playbook document to restart the EC2 instance.

Now, let's select **Lambda function** as the target for the EventBridge:

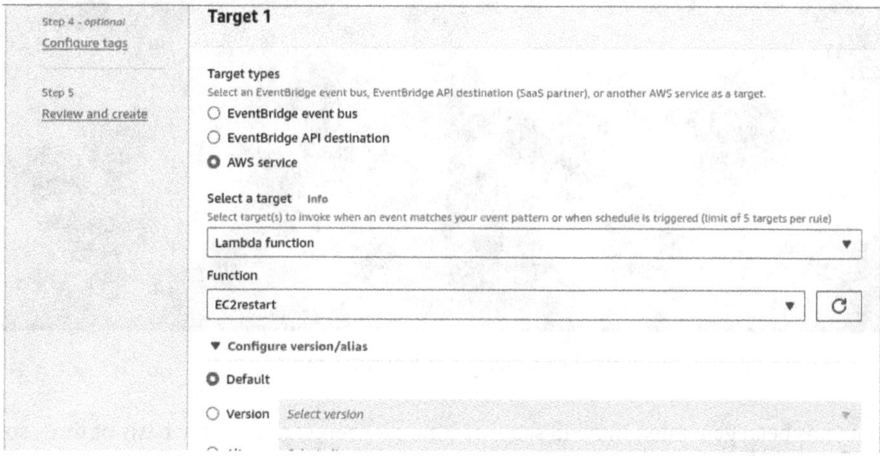

Figure 6.10 – Target Lambda function

9. Keep hitting **Next** until you create the EventBridge rule. When the alarm is triggered, that rule will trigger and run the Lambda function. This will restart the instance and keep doing so until the network input has been restored to acceptable levels.

Now, in this example, we saw an application that is based on an immediate reaction and implementation. This is good if your system is under some sort of attack meant to overwhelm it or to exploit something that you can't patch. However, attacks don't usually come in ones. They are targeted and frequent, constantly trying to find some sort of vulnerability from which to attack your workload. To help understand potential attack patterns and learn more about how your workload handles changes in general, you can use pattern analysis of monitored logs.

Pattern analysis of monitored logs

Monitored logs can give you insights into how an application has performed and if there are some unusual patterns detected within the timeline. For example, **distributed denial-of-service (DDoS)** attacks usually create a pattern of inexplicable high CPU usage in an application. It essentially causes the application to suffer from fake loads, which affect the actual loads in the application.

So, in order to detect these attacks, we must have an algorithm that can historically analyze your workload and potentially find such attacks. To find these patterns, Python has some great data science libraries.

Public datasets of server logs are difficult to find, but they can be recreated fairly easily. For this example, I will use the public dataset mocking service **Mockaroo**. It lets you create a dataset of 1,000 rows for free. I will only create a dataset with the CPU utilization and the timestamp.

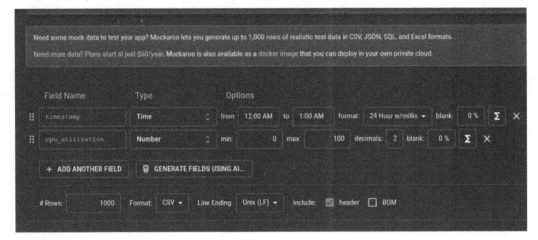

Figure 6.11 – Generating a mock dataset

Once the data has been generated, we will see that it hasn't been sorted on the basis of time, so that is an extra step that we will add to our script. We will write our script using Google Colab. So, let's get started:

1. First, install the `pandas` and `matplotlib` libraries. They are usually there already, but this step helps in other notebook applications:

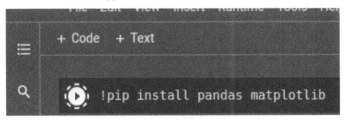

Figure 6.12 – Installation command

2. Next, upload the CSV that Mockaroo created to Colab. To do this, click the folder icon in the side panel and then click the first icon within it to upload the data:

Figure 6.13 – Uploading mock data

You will see here that I have already uploaded my data.

3. Now, the next step is to read the data using pandas to create a dataframe and order it by time, because the mock data in the CSV was not pre-arranged in a sequence.

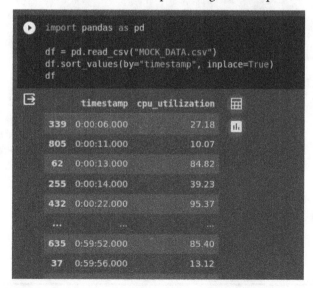

Figure 6.14 – Table for CPU utilization

4. Now, to find the pattern in the data, we can begin by visualizing the data. Let's visualize this data as a linear plot with the timestamp as the x-axis and CPU utilization as the y-axis:

```python
import matplotlib.pyplot as plt

plt.figure(figsize=(20, 20))
plt.plot(df['timestamp'], df['cpu_utilization'], label='Data')

plt.title('Plot for CPU utilization')
plt.xlabel('Time')
plt.ylabel('CPU utilization')
plt.grid(True)
plt.legend()

plt.show()
```

Figure 6.15 – Code to plot CPU utilization

Now, the plot is sort of random, being randomly generated and all, so the diagram is not necessarily representative of what the actual diagram would look like.

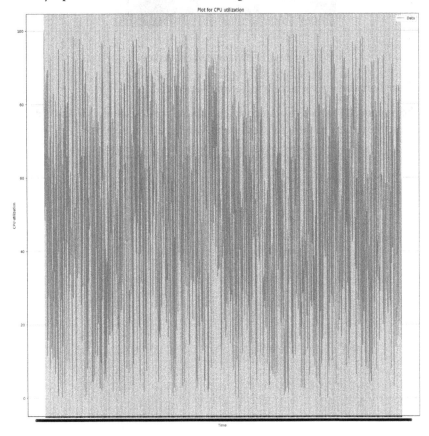

Figure 6.16 – Diagram plotting CPU utilization over time

So, this looks random, but that's fine as it's simply meant to be a representative of a bar graph over time. Let's refine the dataset a little to create anomalies.

5. So, we are going to modify the dataset to have a constant utilization rate somewhere in the middle:

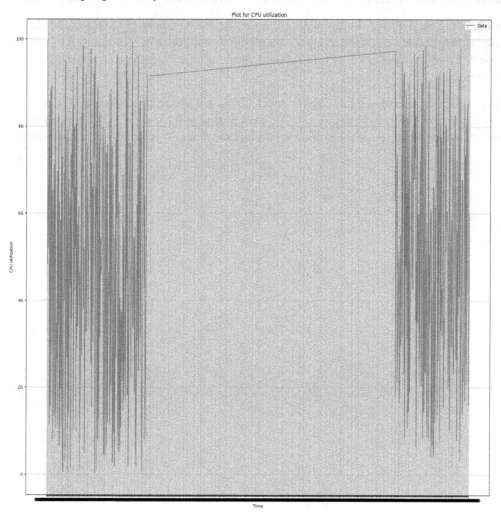

Figure 6.17 – Chart for modified dataset

This is a little ridiculous, but I believe it illustrates the point of constant uptime. Most systems, when they are stable, do not have this kind of utilization. If your service is getting this kind of data, it either indicates a sudden spike of success or a DDoS attack. More often than not, it is the latter. So, if you find this kind of spike in your monitoring data, it is worth investigating.

Summary

In this chapter, you have hopefully learned a thing or two about security. I also hope that you have figured out how to build your infrastructure in such a way that all of the access keys you use are secured.

In addition to this, you have also learned some methods (among hundreds of thousands) that can be used to help secure your infrastructure. You may have also gotten some insights into how you can use data to drive the response to incidents and also find better insight into certain incidents and their properties.

So, friends, I hope you enjoyed this chapter, which is all about security. I tried my best to explain a couple of concepts to you and I hope you found it interesting, at least. But now, it is time to flip the page and move on to the next chapter, where we will talk about one of my favorite topics: **automation**.

7

Automating Tasks

The goal of the future is full unemployment. So that we can play.

– Arthur C Clarke

This is probably going to be my favorite chapter. Seriously, once you have drunk the sweet nectar of automation, you won't look back. Well, I guess I'm getting ahead of myself. I will start with the concept of time. The only way you control your destiny, the way you live, and what you do is by controlling your own time, by choosing what you do. And to do that, you need to choose what it is that you do with your time.

All human advancement correlates to doing something in a way that requires fewer and fewer workers and continually decreased effort so that greater effort can then be applied elsewhere. All of this defines the concept of automation. It is inventing ways to reduce time investment in the boring stuff so that you can move on and do more exciting or engaging stuff.

Human beings invented agriculture so that they wouldn't have to spend so much time hunting and gathering food. They could grow their own; the food, in many ways, grew itself (automatically some would say) and a little bit of tinkering led to the food that we eat to this day. The creation of farming automated the food creation process, which kickstarted towns and owning property and most of human civilization.

During the Industrial Revolution, the automation of manufacturing processes resulted in cheap, mass-manufactured goods being brought to practically every household. The ability to create identical goods that were of high quality and worked perfectly was revolutionary. It meant that the labor required to create something was greatly reduced meaning that that labor could be focused elsewhere. The invention of the steam engine, electricity, and motor vehicles also reduced labor in a number of different areas while saving time in many others.

Around the World in Eighty Days by *Jules Verne* was a novel symbolizing how far human innovation had gone toward shortening trips around the globe. Within a hundred years of the publication of that novel, man had conquered all forms of terrestrial travel, making the book trivial. The next question that was then asked was how the human mind could be made faster and more automated. This is where computers came in. Computers turn the human brain into the most efficient tool in the world. They have automated a lot of our menial mental workload, allowing the human brain to be freed up for more leisurely tasks.

However, this process is a never-ending one. There is always some way to get better and to do something faster and without taking up any more of one's focus. In the DevOps field, we have made it into one of our core principles because of how much innovation, creativity, and coming up with new ideas are valued in the field of technology. You cannot stay in the same place you were yesterday. You must automate and move on.

And that is what this chapter will be about. It will concern *Automating the Boring Stuff with Python* (another great Python book by *Al Sweigart*) and letting you use your mind and your creativity to maximum utilization. You do not want to be stuck in the causal loop of doing the same upload, running the same script manually, or fixing that recurring server issue manually even though it only takes about 5 seconds but logging into it takes 10 minutes. All of these are problems where automation is the answer.

In this chapter, you will learn about the following:

- Automation of server maintenance within the server and outside of it
- Automation of container creation through managed services and otherwise
- Automated launching of a playbook using Google Forms

Automating server maintenance and patching

I once had a friend whose only job most days was to wait for a website to go down, check why it had gone done, and do one of two things or commands that he had been given to bring it back up again. I had another friend whose job was to manually restart an NGINX server whenever it went down. I once met a man whose job largely involved just downloading CSVs from one place, putting them somewhere else, and clicking a start button. Now, to some of you, that might sound like a swell gig (to me, it doesn't sound half bad either), but the thing about it is that it is a waste of time for both that individual's employers and that individual themselves. There is no growth or improvement for either, and in my experience of life, that is a waste of human life.

In the coming samples, we are going to see how we can maintain multiple instance fleets based on a series of common commands and then we are going to find a way to patch an OS after we have discovered the type of OS it is running. We are going to do all of this with the help of Python.

Sample 1: Running fleet maintenance on multiple instance fleets at once

Maintaining a server involves a lot of work – a lot of repetitive work. This is why server maintenance was initially automated. It minimizes human error and also makes sure that the process occurs the same way every time. A fleet of servers works similarly. It is just about using the automation script for all of them since they are copies of an original server. But what about multiple instance fleets with different needs? Here, Python can be of assistance. All you need to do is associate each fleet with the correct script for maintaining it. This can allow you to manage multiple fleets over multiple clouds if you want to. So, without further ado, let's see how we can do that:

1. Let's first write the code for AWS instances to find the instances that are running:

```
import boto3

ec2_client = boto3.client('ec2')
response = ec2.describe_instances(Filters=[{'Name': 'instance-
state-name', 'Values': ['running']}])
aws_instances = response['Reservations']
```

This will give us a list of instances from EC2 to use. You can use a number of identifiers to define your fleet. You can even use a pre-defined system manager fleet.

2. Let's now do the same thing for Google Cloud Compute Engine instances:

```
from google.cloud import compute_v1

instance_client = compute_v1.InstancesClient()
request = compute_v1.AggregatedListInstancesRequest()
request.project = "ID of GCP project that you are using"
gcp_instances= instance_client.aggregated_list(request=request,
filter="status:RUNNING")
```

In the **Google Cloud Platform** (**GCP**) code, there are a few differences because you need to specify the GCP project ID and you have to define the request to the API along with the API itself.

3. Now, let's find a command to run through these instances. It can be any placeholder command. You can later use the commands you want for it:

```
command = "sudo reboot"
#for AWS
ssm.send_command(InstanceIds=aws_instances,
DocumentName="<Whatever you want to name it>",
    Comment='Run a command on an EC2 instance',
    Parameters={
        'commands': [command]
    }
```

```
)
#for Google Cloud
import os
import subprocess
from google.oauth2 import service_account
from googleapiclient import discovery
# Load the service account credentials
service_account_file = '<file_name_here>.json'
credentials = service_account.Credentials.from_service_account_
file(
    service_account_file, scopes=['https://www.googleapis.com/
auth/cloud-platform']
)

# Create a Compute Engine API client
compute = discovery.build('compute', 'v1',
credentials=credentials)

# Get the public IP address of the VM instance
request = compute.instances().get(project="<your_
project>",instance="your_instance_name")
response = request.execute()
public_ip = response['networkInterfaces'][0]['accessConfigs'][0]
['natIP']
# SSH into the VM instance and run the command
ssh_command = f'gcloud compute ssh {instance_name} --zone {zone}
--command "{command}"'

try:
    subprocess.run(ssh_command, shell=True, check=True)
except subprocess.CalledProcessError:
    print("Error executing SSH command.")
```

The preceding code for GCP and AWS differs a bit because of the way that the APIs have been developed for it. However, they both will produce the result of executing an SSH command on their servers.

So, if we iterate through the lists that we previously produced through the function to update them with a command, we can make a mass change or update to our entire instance fleet.

This method is good for a generic fleet where we presume that all the OS are the same or that they run the same commands. But what if we were in an environment where the OS could be different? How would we then go about using commands? In the next section, we will explore this possibility.

Sample 2: Centralizing OS patching for critical updates

OS are like any brand, really. Well, at least among most of the tech community, it's like Coke and Pepsi – except if Coke or Pepsi was your belligerent pet who constantly wanted your attention and needed maintenance. What I'm trying to say is the flavor you want is your preference. But, if you're going to share a fridge, there will probably be flavors that you are not familiar with. So, the fridge needs to be accommodating to all flavors. This is a rather long-winded analogy, but you'll get what I'm saying as we keep going. This fridge sorting is even more difficult (and important) when dealing with servers, which can have a similar diversity. To patch OS correctly, we must first understand which OS we are operating on. Then, we need to apply the correct command to ensure that the patching is done correctly for that OS. This again is where Python comes in. It has libraries that can do both and when combined can be a powerful asset.

Let's start off with the process of patching a single OS. We will use a **Debian OS** with the apt package manager for this case:

```
import subprocess
update_command = "sudo apt update && sudo apt upgrade -y"
subprocess.run(update_command, shell=True)
```

As you can see in the code, it's simply a matter of running an update command using Python's subprocess module, which once again reinforces the incredible connection that Python has with the OS that it is working on.

But this is just for a Debian Linux instance. What would happen if that instance was, say, Red Hat or CentOS? What if the script had to function for both? Then we just need to add an additional library: platform. This library will give us the knowledge we need to distinguish between the platforms and the ability to write all the patch code in one script:

```
import subprocess
import platform
def update_os():
    system = platform.system().lower()
    if system == 'linux' or system == 'linux2':
        if 'debian' in platform.linux_distribution()[0].lower() or
'ubuntu' in platform.linux_distribution()[0].lower():
            update_command = "sudo apt update && sudo apt upgrade -y"
        else:
            update_command = "sudo dnf update -y"   subprocess.
run(update_command, shell=True)

    elif system == 'windows':
        update_command = 'powershell -Command "Start-Service -Name
wuauserv; Get-WindowsUpdate; Install-WindowsUpdate;"'
        subprocess.run(update_command, shell=True)
```

```
if __name__ == "__main__":
    update_os()
```

The preceding code works for Debian distributions, the latest RedHat distributions (older ones use yum instead), and Windows PowerShell. The script will determine which OS you are currently running on and run an update accordingly. Since the command can be modified, you can change it and make the update whatever you'd like it to be. You can also add on OS such as Darwin for macOS or more obscure Linux distributions.

You may now be thinking *"Patching an OS is going to break my server."* Fair enough. That can happen a lot, especially for older dependencies. And in the case of a lot of Linux servers, the latest versions of OS can take years to become approved server versions. If you feel that this is a hassle, then maybe you should try out containers. There's plenty of opportunity there for the automation enthusiast as well.

Automating container creation

Containers – in the eyes of many – are magic. You can put all the stuff you need for a smaller application or a section of a larger application into an environment solely catered to it where it can function on its own. It's like creating a separate planet where polar bears can live in their native environment forever free from the terrors of global warming. In this way, containers are amazing since they can help maintain nearly extinct technologies in environments that can sustain them. That is truly magic. But casting the spell is rather bothersome, which is why we automate stuff.

Sample 1: Creating containers based on a list of requirements

Containers change between initialization and stoppage based on changes in the state of the files and configurations within the container. Capturing an image from this changed container will give an image that has several layers added on top of the initial layer. This is a way to create custom containers as well. This can be useful when the containers that we find are largely what our requirements are but are not exactly our requirements. We can add a few steps (and a few layers) to make our container just as we would like it. We can then turn this into an image, which can then be replicated for other containers. We can do all of this with Python (big surprise, amirite?):

1. Let's once again start off with some simple code to start a container based on an image:

```
import docker

client = docker.from_env()
container = client.containers.run('ubuntu:latest', detach=True,
command='/bin/bash')
container_id = container.id
print("Container ID:" + container_id)
```

This set of commands will run a container containing the latest version of Ubuntu. It will also give us the ID of the container, which will be important in the next step. This will be our starting point.

2. Now, let's add on to it:

```
#you can put in any command you want as long as it works
new_command = "ls"
new_image = client.containers.get(container_id).commit()
new_image_tag = "<whatever_you_want>:latest"
new_container = client.containers.run(new_image_tag,
detach=True, command=new_command)
```

Now, we have a new container that has the new command added on top of everything else in Ubuntu. This container is different from the original one but built upon the original.

3. Next, we need to export this image for later use:

```
image = client.images.get("<whatever_you_want>:latest")
image.save("<insert_file_path_here>")
```

This will save your image in the desired file path. Putting all of this code together, we get the following:

```
import docker

#Step 1: Intialize and run a container
client = docker.from_env()
container = client.containers.run('ubuntu:latest', detach=True,
command='/bin/bash')
container_id = container.id
print("Container ID:" + container_id)
#Step 2: Add a layer
#you can put in any command you want as long as it works
new_command = "ls"
new_image = client.containers.get(container_id).commit()
new_image_tag = "<whatever_you_want>:latest"
new_container = client.containers.run(new_image_tag,
detach=True, command=new_command)
#Step 3: Export layered container as an image
image = client.images.get("<whatever_you_want>:latest")
image.save("<insert_file_path_here>")
```

The full code gives us the complete picture and shows us that all of this can be done in just a few short steps. Adding layers simply means adding more commands. You can even start with an empty template that has nothing in it if you want.

This is all good if you are creating individual customized images, but another complicated aspect of containers is orchestrating multiple containers together to perform a task. This requires a lot of work and is why Kubernetes was created. Kubernetes clusters – even though they simplify container orchestration a lot – can be quite a handful. This is another area of container automation, then, that Python can be useful for.

Sample 2: Spinning up Kubernetes clusters

I will start off with a personal note: when I first got into Kubernetes, it was probably the hardest thing in the world for me. I came from a development background and something like container orchestration was completely alien to me at the time. Kubernetes was born out of a very complicated need because of the rise in popularity of microservices. It was created to make life simpler for larger projects that were a mishmash of smaller projects. When it finally clicked for me, I realized how important Kubernetes was. It didn't stop me from still being confused, though. So, I went to the coding well and it turns out there are a bunch of resources for guys like me. Once again, Python was a big help.

Creating a Kubernetes cluster usually involves using it in a cloud service. For this exercise, we are going to write code for setting up clusters in Google Cloud and Microsoft Azure:

```python
from google.cloud import container_v1
# Specify your project ID and cluster details
project_id = "<YOUR_PROJECT_ID>"
zone = "<PREFERRED_ZONE>"
cluster_name = "<YOUR_CLUSTER>"
node_pool_name = 'default-pool'
node_count = 1
    client = container_v1.ClusterManagerClient()

    # Create a GKE cluster
    cluster = container_v1.Cluster(
        name=cluster_name,
        initial_node_count=node_count,
        node_config=container_v1.NodeConfig(
            machine_type='n1-standard-2',
        ),
    )
    operation = client.create_cluster(project_id, zone, cluster)
```

This operation will create a Kubernetes cluster in your Google Cloud project. Now let's look at a way to do it in Azure:

```
from azure.mgmt.containerservice.models import ManagedCluster,
ManagedClusterAgentPoolProfile
resource_group = '<RESOURCE_GROUP_HERE>'
cluster_name = '<CLUSTER_NAME_HERE>'
location = '<LOCATION_HERE>'
 agent_pool_profile = ManagedClusterAgentPoolProfile(
    name='agentpool',
    count=3,
    vm_size='Standard_DS2_v2',
)
 aks_cluster = ManagedCluster(location=location, kubernetes_
version='1.21.0', agent_pool_profiles = [agent_pool_profile])
aks_client.managed_clusters.begin_create_or_update(resource_group,
cluster_name, aks_cluster).result()
```

This creation code is fairly standard as well; it is simply a change in terminology. This is probably not the most efficient way to write code for this function (that will come later with Infrastructure as Code), but it gets the job done.

A lot of what we have looked at so far is gibberish to the layman, and sometimes the layman is the one most frequently operating resources. So let's now look at a process that can be a blueprint for automating more complex processes to involve the layman more in the resource creation process.

Automated launching of playbooks based on parameters

Most of the time, even the most basic tasks when automated can become difficult to understand. If you have to automate or trigger multiple tasks, the complexity starts to increase. Not everyone can understand them, and it shouldn't be the job of everyone to understand them. That is why even a lot of modern servers have user interfaces that make the processing of information easier for many.

However, in many cases, even this level of abstraction isn't enough. It may be necessary to create a tool in which users can simply enter their inputs and the server handles the creation of complex workflows and resources automatically. In short, you can make playbooks with parameters that will create resources based on an overview given to it by someone who would like the creation of the resource but does not want to bother with the intricacies behind it (in most places, these rather whimsical folk are called customers). Let's see how to do that:

1. We will start by making a Google Form (yes, seriously). Go to forms.google.com and click on the big plus (+) button.

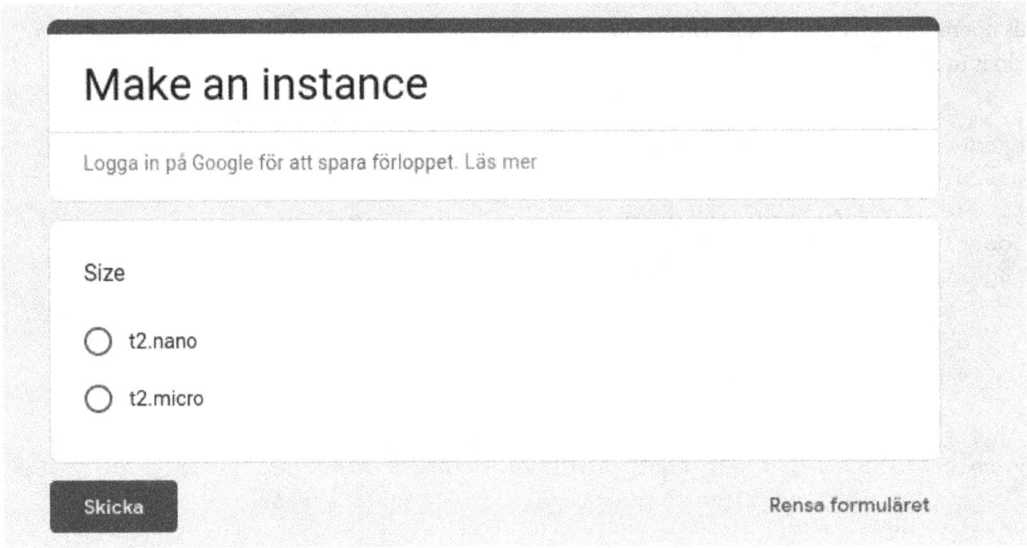

Figure 7.1 – Instance selection

It's a simple Google Form for two different sizes of EC2 instances.

2. Now, we are going to write a Google Apps Script script and an AWS Lambda function:

```python
import boto3

ec2 = boto3.client('ec2')

def lambda_handler(event, context):
    instance_size = event['instance_size']

    response = ec2.run_instances(
        ImageId='<INSERT_AMI_HERE>',
        InstanceType=instance_size,
        MinCount=1,
        MaxCount=1,
        SecurityGroupIds=['<INSERT_SECURITY_GROUP_HERE'],
        SubnetId='<INSERT_SUBNET_HERE>'
    )

    return response
```

This Lambda function takes an input consisting of the size of the EC2 instance to be created and then creates that instance. We can define an endpoint for it using the Lambda URL or the API gateway.

3. Once this function and this endpoint have been made, you can then call the endpoint from Apps Script and make the trigger and the input from the form. In the form editor, click on the three dots at the top right and click on **Script editor**:

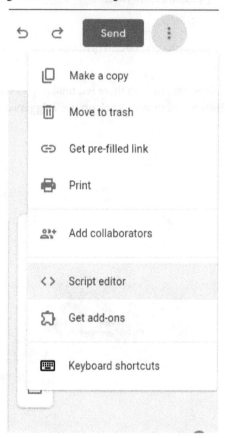

Figure 7.2 – Accessing Script editor

4. You can now write the API script in what is essentially JavaScript:

```
function submitForm(e) {
var responses = e.values;
var size = responses[0];
var apiUrl = '<YOUR_LAMBDA_URL>';
var requestData = {
'instance_size': size,
```

```
};


var requestBody = JSON.stringify(requestData);
var options = {
'method': 'get',
'contentType': 'application/json',
'payload': requestBody,
};
var response = UrlFetchApp.fetch(apiUrl, options);
}
```

This will run the Lambda function, though there is a final step to trigger it by adding a trigger. On the left pane of the Apps Script project, click on the **Triggers** option.

Figure 7.3 – Calling Lambda using Apps Script

5. At the bottom right, click on **Add Trigger**, which will open the form to create a trigger where you can define all the necessary parameters:

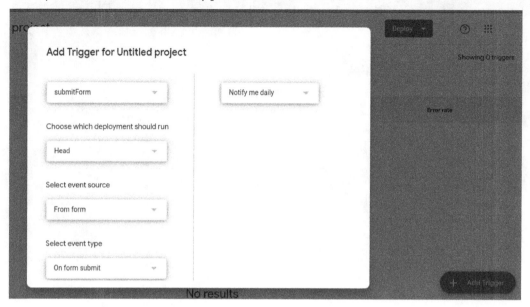

Figure 7.4 – Adding a trigger for when the form is submitted…

Here, we can add the source of the event, and the function, and select the event type.

In doing so, we will create a workflow that will trigger a function when form data is submitted and use the data provided to the function to trigger an API URL.

And there you have it, that's one way to connect all of the machinations that happen behind the scenes in a Lambda function with a simple Google Form.

Summary

In this chapter, we discussed the beauty of automation along with the means to achieve it. We learned how to automate virtual machine maintenance and container operations. We even learned how to add a layer of automation on top of that that would allow us to get people who are significantly less in the know involved in our process. Automation is a good thing. People will often believe otherwise and fear the automation of a lot of tasks, but the point of automation is to ensure that it is easier for people to live their lives. A life is not meant for boring repetitive tasks, it is meant for exploration. Automation is key to free up time for exploration. You control your life by controlling your time. Automation lets you do that.

In the next chapter, we will discuss the events that drive not only automation but most DevOps infrastructure in general. We will look into event-driven architecture and use cases where it is advantageous, as well as – of course – how Python can help.

## 8

Understanding Event-Driven Architecture

Al freir de los huevos lo vera. (It will be seen in the frying of the eggs.)

– Miguel de Cervantes (Don Quixote)

In any application, everything can be divided into **events**. Events are triggered either by some interaction with an external actor (either another application or a user) or by other events. An application is basically the triggering of multiple sequences of events to perform some sort of function. Google Drive, for example, is an application, and its function is just storage. Of course, this is an oversimplification and there are a lot of things that go into storing, organizing, and serving files, but that is the basic gist of it. It functions based on a series of events, each of which comes from a certain source.

Now, different events require different technologies, frameworks, and libraries within the system to interact with each other in perfect harmony. When this harmony is naturally achieved, it is a thing of beauty. However, it almost never is. There is always some sort of bottleneck or some custom part that needs to be made, and it almost always concerns the data that comes from an event. You can have the perfect tool for your system but it's useless if it cannot process the events that it receives. So, what conclusion did all the brainiacs come up with when they realized this? They figured out that there are no perfect systems, nor are there perfect events. What is required is a system that is not tightly bound to any sort of data processing, a system that can take a bit of human error. Not a less precise system, but one that works with the realities of the situation that it has been put in: a loosely coupled system.

Systems such as these are built so that they take events from multiple sources and process them for output in the simplest way possible. They break down every single event and event handler into their own components. These components then interact with other components based entirely on the input they receive and the output they give. If it can be helped, no component is fully dependent on the other. A system like this may seem inefficient, but when the goal is reliability in an unreliable world, it becomes quite appealing.

So, now that I have finished my customary monologue, let's look at how to break down that unnecessary monolith. In this chapter, you will learn about the following:

- The basic concepts behind and use of **Publisher/Subscriber** (**Pub/Sub**) architecture
- The general concept behind **loosely coupled architecture** and why Python is already well suited for it
- The effective industry standard for breaking down a monolithic application into smaller loose components

There will also be some Python, as well as some other things. In fact, that is exactly what I am about to get into right now.

Technical requirements

The following may help you in fully benefiting from this chapter:

- Python installed with the `confluent-kafka` library
- An AWS account
- An open mind (figuratively, not literally; well, if you want to do so literally, it's fine but I don't recommend it)

Introducing Pub/Sub and employing Kafka with Python using the confluent-kafka library

Before we get into what the modern Pub/Sub model is, let's go into a bit of detail about the technology that made this field possible: **Apache Kafka**, the third most famous Kafka after Franz and *Kafka on the Shore*. Originally designed for use in LinkedIn (a great website), it was made open source in early 2011. The concept behind it was pretty simple: there is a log of information and events that any number of systems can consume, and data can be published to the log for consumption by these systems. Sound simple enough? Well, it is now, but it took some thinking to come up with it. But this is the system that is responsible for most modern data infrastructure that we see today. Have you ever gotten a notification on your phone? It is because of this library. Have you ever made a contactless payment with your phone or credit card? Chances are, Kafka's in there. Ever gotten a notification for a YouTube video? Definitely Kafka.

In most cases where raw unadulterated Kafka is used, the distributor of information is called the **producer** and the receiver of said information is called the **consumer**. In most modern nomenclature, as well as with most cloud services, they are instead called the **publisher** and the **subscriber**.

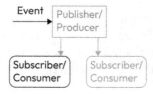

Figure 8.1 – Events processing with the Pub/Sub model

Before we dive into the use of Kafka and Python in DevOps, we must first look at a sample usage of Kafka with Python using the `confluent-kafka` library:

1. Let's first install the library using `pip`:

    ```
    pip install confluent-kafka
    ```

2. Now, as mentioned before, Kafka is divided between a producer and a consumer. So, let's first write a piece of code that creates a producer:

    ```
    from confluent_kafka import Producer
    import socket

    conf = {'bootstrap.servers': '<host_name>:9092',
            'client.id': socket.gethostname()}

    producer = Producer(conf)
    ```

3. This code will configure a producer. Replace `host_name` with the name of an Apache Kafka cluster (online or locally). Next, we need to use the configured producer to send some data. Let's look at that code now:

    ```
    producer.produce(topic, key="key", value="value")
    ```

    Here, `topic` is the location where the publisher or producer will distribute their content for it to be consumed. The `key` and the `value` elements are the keys and values that will be distributed by the producer.

4. Let's now add some code for a consumer that will pick up messages sent by the producer:

    ```
    from confluent_kafka import Consumer

    conf = {'bootstrap.servers': '<host_name>:9092',
            'group.id': '<group_id_here>',
            'auto.offset.reset': 'smallest'}

    consumer = Consumer(conf)
    ```

The consumer now listens on the same host that the producer sends messages on. So, when the producer produces a message, the consumer can consume it. When a consumer is subscribed to a topic, that consumer is constantly listening to the message at certain intervals. Once the message arrives, it will begin the process of interpreting the message and sending it to the appropriate location.

5.   To have the consumer continually listen to the producer for messages, we can place it in a loop:

```
while True:
msg = consumer.poll(timeout=1.0)
if msg is None: continue
break
#If msg is not None, it will break the loop and the message will
be processed
```

This is simply understanding the way that these Pub/Sub mechanisms work. In application, it is much easier since some sort of mechanism to perform this will already be provided for you. This is, however, a good way to learn how to make custom Pub/Sub structures if you want to, and to just understand Pub/Sub structures in general.

Here's what the key takeaway from this should be: this is how the world works. Exactly like this. Most of the things that come to your phone come from this. Most of the things that go out of your phone go to this. It's also true on a more fundamental level as well, as we will see in the next section.

Understanding the importance of events and consequences

Alright, so now you are in on the secret. Everything is push and pull. People just toss data out there and hope it hits something. And if you've also realized that that is the most effective approach toward growth and development, kudos to you. If you haven't, well, we are about to go into a little story time.

I currently live in Uppsala, Sweden, and for quite a while, I thought I was the only person from Nepal who lived here. Now, Uppsala is a big town by Swedish standards and a lot of students from all over the world live here as well. But, even if Nepalese people lived here, how would I have known them? Something that specific is very hard to find, even in this day and age. But then, the most remarkable set of coincidences (some may even say events, eh?) happened, which brought me into contact with other people from Nepal. I only realized just how remarkable they were once I backtracked through all of them.

I had just recently gotten a job offer (the one that I currently have) in Stockholm and I was getting on the train to Stockholm to iron out the details. On the train, I met a friend of mine with whom I collaborate on projects at the student union in Uppsala. In fact, we had met just the other day to discuss those projects. I saw him and sat down next to him, and I saw that he was with two other friends. One of them was a teaching assistant on a project that I had to submit the very next day. That was cool, but that wasn't even the most important event that happened on the train. His other friend and I got to talking and, through him, I got the number of another Nepalese person who was also living in Uppsala. What kismet! Through that person, I have actually managed to find almost a dozen others who live in the same town as me, who have come on the same journey.

So, here's the thing: I skipped to the end of this story because, in a way, that's how we live our lives, trying to finish something up and get to the end of the story to begin a new one. It is how we read, how we consume content, and basically, how we behave socially. But, over time, I contemplated the story, and I thought back to the set of events that had brought me up to that point, so let's backtrack (and I promise there is a satisfying conclusion to this that isn't just me bragging about my luck):

- I met my friend who introduced me to his friend on the student union developer team
- I joined that team to try and make some new friends in Uppsala, but the information for that came from a WhatsApp group that I joined based on a recommendation from another friend from my faculty
- I became friends with him before we even joined the faculty because we ended up on a student nation tour (look up Uppsala student nations for a fun and interesting read)
- I joined that tour because of the recommendation that I got on my first day in Uppsala during my orientation

But this is the saner half of the event tree that led to this event. The other half is even more interesting:

- I was on that train because I went to sign a job contract.
- I got the offer for that job because I made a post about having all 11 Google Cloud certifications on the Google forums, and the company that I currently work for just happened to notice.
- I made that post exclusively because I got all 11 of those certifications. I got the last one on the day before I left for Sweden. Had I only gotten 10, I wouldn't have made it.
- I got those certifications largely as a sort of reinforcement of the knowledge that I wanted to deliver with this book.
- I got the offer for this book from my publisher after applying for it based on the link that I found in one of their other books, which was a Google Cloud examination book.

So, in a roundabout way, writing this book helped me secure the job I have today, and it eventually led to me finding more Nepalese people in Uppsala. If you couldn't be bothered with all of that, let me show it to you visually:

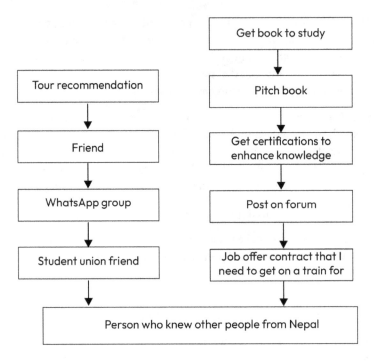

Figure 8.2 – The events that drove a part of my life

The events in our lives lead to the most extraordinary circumstances, and this was just one of the events that came about from this whole saga. Several other remarkable things happened through all of this that made me realize that the true consequences of our actions are truly unpredictable and yet, most of the time, a lot better or at least more exciting than anything we could have possibly planned.

Self-indulgent? Probably. But that is the magic of DevOps. Conforming to tight structures and solid preconceived notions leads to fear and stunts growth. They hide and overshadow opportunities that spontaneity brings. There is no room to find, discover, and fail. Yes, fail, because in something so tightly packed as a monolith, failure can be disastrous. In something loosely coupled, failure is simply a growth opportunity. You can move pieces in and out and iterate to your best possible version. You may look at my story and say that a lot of it is luck and coincidence – for example, in finding the exact person I needed on the train or just happening to have my forum post viewed – but luck is simply an amalgamation of one's sustained attempts. People sometimes get lucky once or twice, but people who are not afraid to fail and who go with the flow are found to be lucky a lot more. God hates a coward.

So, switching gears to something a little less philosophical, loosely coupled architecture is a sort of framework you can use to achieve this kind of meaningful event-based system in your workload. This entire passage was initially supposed to be the next section before it took a life of its own (spontaneity, amirite?). So, let's dive into the actual nitty-gritty now and see what we can find.

Exploring loosely coupled architecture

Alright, in a vacuum, loosely coupled architecture seems like a bad idea. You disperse your components so much that there is no rhyme or reason as to how any information gets from one place to another. You can't count any sort of consistent time for all your data to collate into one place for the thing you want to happen to actually happen.

However, there are a few factors that make loosely coupled architecture so effective in a practical setting. These factors are both philosophical and architectural. Firstly, no matter how well you design a system, it will fail somewhere at some time. The loosely coupled architecture allows the system to fail gracefully and to recover from failures in a way that doesn't affect other components and users of the system. Because each component is isolated, these components can be identified after a single failure (a lot of the time, a clone component will succeed). This failure can be logged and detected and the correct parties can be notified without any interruption to the system. The failed component will not disrupt activities and it is not considered to be a bad thing. In fact, failure teaches us the weaknesses and shortcomings of the system, which can then be worked on quickly because you are only working on that isolated component.

The next factor comes from availability. Loosely coupled architecture offers small components that are replicated for each individual use. Now, you would say that this is a limit in and of itself since even if you can divide the resources between users, there won't be enough resources to go around. In the past, this would have been true, but with modern applications running on the cloud, there can be infinite provisioning for services that support a loose architecture. You can handle the volume of resources effectively because the scale for the services that can run this kind of architecture is nearly infinite. This results in an environment where an architecture that will provision based on use becomes the optimal architecture. A more tightly coupled architecture might suit more limited means, but that is not the case for scenarios with flexible resources and unknown loads.

Finally, the last factor that puts loosely coupled architecture in the lead is laziness. Yes, laziness. I have found in my life that the leading cause behind my laziness is not the fact that I don't want to do something, but rather because my brain is overwhelmed with useless information about something that I might want to do. I started actually getting somewhere when instead of trying to figure out these minutiae in a way that was ineffective and useless, I just started doing things and figuring them out as I went along. That's basically why loosely coupled architecture is good. There are fewer things to worry about and it is easier to work on. Instead of worrying about every single little thing before you even start implementing the system, you can just start implementing and worry about optimization later. This is perfect for someone like me who uses this approach for practically everything, and it's the same for some of the biggest companies in the world as well. If you've heard of the Toyota way, it essentially follows the same principle: making mistakes and learning from them to get better. You can look it up; I encourage you to. But, in conclusion, this type of architecture is for the lazy, pragmatic developer who is just trying to get somewhere.

For the past several paragraphs, you have endured my philosophical rants, and now we get to the more pragmatic part where I show you stuff and try to reinforce what I ranted about. So, that is what we're going to get into right now. We are going to make a basic application (just a lambda function, actually) that is triggered when an image is uploaded into an S3 bucket, takes the image and resizes it to a standard size, deletes the original image, and replaces it with the resized one:

```python
import os
import tempfile
import boto3
from PIL import Image

s3 = boto3.client('s3')

def lambda_handler(event, context):
    # Get the name of the bucket and the image name when upload is
triggered.
    bucket = event['Records'][0]['s3']['bucket']['name']
    key = event['Records'][0]['s3']['object']['key']

    new_width = 300 #width of image
    new_height = 200 #height of image

    with tempfile.TemporaryDirectory() as tmpdir:
        # Download the original image from S3 into a pre-defined
temporary directory
        download_path = os.path.join(tmpdir, 'original.jpg')

        #download the S3 file into the temporay path
        s3.download_file(bucket, key, download_path)

        with Image.open(download_path) as image:
            image = image.resize((new_width, new_height))

            # Save the resized image in its own path
            resized_path = os.path.join(tmpdir, 'resized.jpg')
            image.save(resized_path)

        # Upload the resized image back to the S3 bucket and delete
the original
        s3.delete_object(Bucket=bucket, Key=key)
        s3.upload_file(resized_path, bucket, key)


    return {
```

```
        'statusCode': 200,
        'body': 'You don't really need this because its not for
people!'
    }
```

This is a simple code for a very simple yet important function. The trigger for the image conversion can be placed either at the lambda function or the S3 bucket itself. If you have ever used one of those online services that convert your PDF to a Microsoft Word document or convert your WAVs into MP3s, they basically run on this concept. Even with a very minimal interface, they can be very effective and quite popular.

Perhaps before reading this book, you may have had the misconception that building some of these services might be difficult. In the world we live in, they are not. Once we have opened these horizons, everything becomes clearer, and one of the things that becomes clearest of all is the ability to move on from the old inefficient ways into newer, simpler ways. Let's look at the path to that transition.

Killing your monolith with the strangler fig

If you oppose killing anything (and I understand), simply change the word/s in your mind to happier ones (such as "sleeping" or "napping"). But the **strangler fig** is being talked about here because it is one of the most prominent methods in the **digital transformation** and/or modernization of applications. You may have heard the term digital transformation and immediately dismissed it as some buzzword, which, fair enough, most of the time when people use that word, it is. But open your eyes and ears for a moment and treat the term for what it actually is: it is changing old things into new things. It is basically changing your system from within while either maintaining the same functionality or increasing functionality. It is the breaking of the monolith into a loosely coupled architecture.

For starters, let's look at the potential structure of a monolithic application:

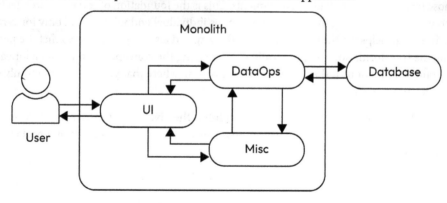

Figure 8.3 – A basic monolith

It's quite crude, but that is basically how most monolithic applications are structured. They have a user interface, which interacts with two different types of operations: operations on the database and generic data operations (**Misc** in the diagram). Even this monolith is rather more divided than regular monoliths since we have given it a separate database. The database can also be directly within the monolith sometimes.

Breaking down this monolith is not just about making it disassociated; it is about making sure that each component can act as an individual entity in case it becomes of use in some other project or in a different way in the same project. But to continue with the breaking down of this monolith, we can keep that going by first removing the miscellaneous functions that require no interaction with the users or the database from the monolith.

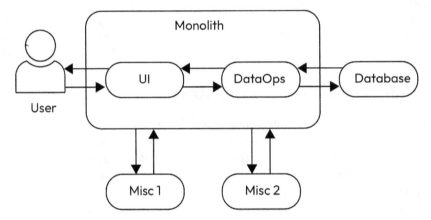

Figure 8.4 – Removing miscellaneous APIs from the monolith

So, this diagram indicates that the separation between the monolith and the miscellaneous functions divides those functions into individual components. This is the foundation of serverless architecture. It is all about exclusively having individual functions as individual endpoints to call only for certain use cases. This stage helps get the easy stuff out of the way and also helps make it so that the people performing the transformation can practically start grasping the concept behind it. It's a lot easier to manage random functions if they are just endpoints somewhere that you can call randomly and modify to suit certain needs.

Now, the next step toward breaking down this monolith is the division of the user interface and the backend portion that performs the data operations. This involves placing an API or a backend for the frontend in between them.

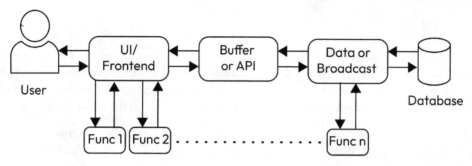

Figure 8.5 – A fully decoupled architecture

The final structure after breaking down the monolith looks like *Figure 8.5*. It's a bit like my consequences diagram but not as foolish. There are a lot of moving parts here, but then again, there are a lot of moving parts in cars too; it's what makes them work. More importantly, let's look at this from the lens of the two things emphasized in this chapter, availability and failure:

- If the user interface for some reason stops loading, it will fall back to a different region. This region will have the same capabilities; if it's further from the user, it might be slower, but it will do the job.

- The API or backend for the frontend can receive calls from multiple user interfaces and can access multiple servers that have access to the database.

- The backend can then simply be there to connect to the database for operations. There is no need for anything there except for queries.

- The database itself becomes more secure due to the layers present and it becomes easier to increase its availability.

- The miscellaneous functions are simply endpoints that can be put in or taken out as it suits the development team.

Well, that is quite the process, isn't it? But it is one that gives results and helps make your application or workload more sustainable and futureproof. It doesn't work for every workload, but it is fantastic in helping older systems use modern technology better.

Summary

In this chapter, you learned about the event-driven architecture that comprises a lot of modern application development. You also, hopefully, learned about actions and their consequences and how important positive actions are to development and your life in general. Lastly, you learned about a way to modernize older applications toward this new philosophy through the use of the strangler fig.

In the next chapter, you will get even more hands-on with Python and learn about the role that Python can play in **CI/CD** (short for **continuous integration/continuous delivery**). It's a fun topic and will help you implement the Python skills and concepts you've been studying in this chapter.

9

Using Python for CI/CD Pipelines

I've missed over 9,000 shots in my career. I've lost almost 300 games. 26 times I've been trusted to take the game-winning shot and missed. I've failed over and over and over again in my life. And that is why I succeed.

– Michael Jordan

In the past, when I was but a young college graduate (some two years ago), the term that kept coming up, right after being taught how to make a website, was **Continuous Integration/Continuous Delivery (CI/CD)**. CI/CD was something that my college course did not teach. Most college courses do not; it is not enough of an academic exercise. However, if you're a DevOps engineer, this is all you'll do. This is your job. And Python is a great tool for doing your job better.

I have often described Python as a great facilitator, that is, as a tool that makes all other tools better. And that is the concept that we will explore further in this chapter. Python is a language that is very kind toward people who make mistakes; trust me, I've made plenty. It has a lot of features that reduce the impact of your mistakes. It also has error messages, which allow the tracing of errors to be simple and effective. If we're talking about actual application development from the perspective of a developer, everyone has their own opinion, which is, to an extent, valid. But as I have talked about throughout this book, Python is significantly ahead in terms of what it can offer DevOps engineers.

So, as we explore how to deliver a journey to our customers, this is what we are going to learn:

- The philosophy and the concepts behind CI/CD and how it has evolved during the course of its creation

- A basic CI/CD task using Python that can help you understand CI/CD, what it brings to the table, and how important its implementation is

- How Python can be used to develop and enhance collaboration within a development team using its flexible nature

- How Python can be used to enhance and automate the most sacred of DevOps traditions: the rollback

To accomplish these tasks, you will require a few tools in your bag. There are a few things that you need to set up before we begin.

Technical requirements

We have a short checklist here of things that you will need in order to follow along with this chapter:

- A GitHub account for use of the book repository
- A Todoist account
- A Microsoft account
- An AWS account
- The ability to tolerate a large amount of sarcasm and bad humor

We also, of course, have an accompanying GitHub repository where you can reference the coding content in this book: `https://github.com/PacktPublishing/Hands-On-Python-for-DevOps/`.

The origins and philosophy of CI/CD

A question that people often ask me is, "You started as a developer; how did you end up where you are?" I've answered this to an extent over several of the sections in this book, but in short, I had to make my way there because of necessity. These days, the people who develop applications are taught how to do so from the start and do not know about all of the rationale behind it, just how to use it. This is fine; there is no need to dive deeper than you want, but know that this was not always the case. Someone had to figure all of this stuff out (several someones, in fact). And I think my personal journey is more reflective of the people who figured this stuff out than your typical modern DevOps trainee. So, I'll start recapping this journey as a short dialog of three scenes of me screaming into the void (let's call it DevOps Doug, that sounds fun). We'll start with CI.

Scene 1 – continuous integration

It was a late night at my home. I was doing my usual 200 push-up, 300 sit-up routine when it dawned on me that I am really good at writing code. This shouldn't have been a revelation, it was pretty obvious in hindsight, but upon making this discovery, I decided – being the generous man that I am – that I wanted to share my coding gift with the world, and so I called my old pal Doug for a little help.

Me: Hello, I'd like some help. I have all of this code and I want to share it with my friends.

Doug: That's easy enough. All you have to do is create, clone, initialize, pull, modify, then push the Git repository. That sounds simple, right?

Me: What's a repository? Why can't I just email my code to them, then they can make the changes and email it back to me?

Doug: Well.....

Thus started a long back and forth and a lot of exposition about what version control is, how repositories work, why you have branches, and what pull requests are. If I started going through all of this, I'd have to write another book.

Doug: Did that answer all your questions?

Me: Yeah, I understand it and I understand why it'd be useful, but why is it the way it is?

Doug: Do more and you'll learn more.

And the journey continued, just like the integration, but much longer and sometimes very boring. We'll skip the boring parts.

So, I started learning more and realized how important version control is. I also realized that there are very few younger developers who actually take the time to completely understand it. Some quit over the fact that they can't. But the purpose of CI is clear. It gives a clear history of the modification of code, and it gives you small increments of improvement, which are added on top of other improvements, creating a history of smaller changes that can be looked at, versioned, and understood. It increases organization and understanding more than anything, but those are the things you need first before increasing your speed.

Now, as I evolved, and my skill sets evolved, so did my curiosity. I started thinking, "Is this actually helping the other people on the project?" So I asked them, and they confirmed that it did. I felt it impolite to ask further (also they probably hadn't looked into it much further either), so I started looking for more advanced material on the internet. This next conversation, about continuous delivery, was rather interesting.

Scene 2 – continuous delivery

A while after I was pushed down the DevOps river by Doug, I found myself facing a roadblock. If it were a physical roadblock, I would have no problem given the 400 crunches and 649 (yes, exactly that much) pull-ups I did every day. But this roadblock existed in the realm of computers, and it had a toll booth that rejected any code that didn't meet its requirements. Tired of the automatic rejection of my code, I decided to speak to the toll booth attendant, and lo and behold, I found that it was my old friend Doug.

Me: How'd you get here Doug?

Doug: I was always here.

Me: (Visibly confused) Okay... So, whenever I push my code, it updates the test version of the application?

Doug: That is correct, but only if your code passes testing and deploys successfully. Otherwise, it reverts to the older version of the project and tells you what went wrong.

Me: Okay, can't you just take my word for it?

Doug: I'd love to, but the last time we did that, a zebra came flying out of the server room and started biting people. Zebras are mean.

Me: How did a Zebra…

Doug: That's not the point. The point is that this system doesn't just exist to launch stuff, alright? It's there because it simplifies and secures things for everybody. Once a dev pushes the code, it's over for them. If that code gives out an error, they resume work on it. DevOps people just exist to make that process as easy as possible.

Me: Alright, is that easy to set up?

Doug: Nope.

This is the part with a montage of me learning all of the testing and security principles and how to push code, create approval workflows, and a lot of other things that you've seen in this book. It's not an easy journey by any means, but a rewarding one.

Me: Okay, that's all right. Right?

Doug: Define *all*.

Me: (Sighs) Alright, what's left?

Doug: Do more and you'll learn more.

Thus, the journey continued in earnest, revealing even more questions each time. It was honestly pretty boring. But I soon realized that there was a reason for that...

Well, after the truth was revealed to me, I realized that this actually was the way. A way created through trial and error to find out what works and what doesn't. A way based on real-life problems and their solutions. A more pragmatic way that brought order from chaos. But I also realized that there is such a thing as too much order (we call it bureaucracy if a government does it). There were a lot of necessary steps, but they generated a few unnecessary ones every time something was changed. The process needed to adapt to itself. An interesting concept. And it needed to do so while also delivering value. But to innovate, you must automate. And that is the story of continuous deployment.

Scene 3 – continuous deployment

One fine day, I was sitting in my office, going through my regular routine, drinking some coffee, answering a few emails, and pushing a little bit of code, when I suddenly felt a chill down my spine, like someone was about to come in and turn my life upside down...

Doug: Hey!

Me: Doug! How'd you get in here? That door was locked.

Doug: I am a figment of your imagination; you'll never get away from me. What're you up to?

Me: (Pushing aside that disturbing thought) Well, alright. I have created this lovely pipeline that I am pushing code into. I've worked on it for the past three months. Now I'm going to release it into production.

Doug: You haven't made a release in a full week? What do you think you're doing?

Me: My job...?

Doug: Well, I thought so. That's bad. Get this through your thick skull, kid. If you're doing your job, then you're doing a bad job.

Me: Whose job should I be doing then?

Doug: Not yours.

Me: ☹

Doug: Your job is to automate your job, to make sure that as little is left to human judgment as possible. You must become an artist, striving to paint your masterpiece with as few strokes of the brush as possible. You have now entered the realm of continuous deployment.

Me: If I deploy continuously, when do I develop?

Doug: That's the trick: you don't deploy your app. You create a deployment that constantly deploys it for you.

Me: What? What if I get it wrong?

Doug: That is the other trick: don't be afraid of getting it wrong. That's the success behind DevOps and the CI/CD process; you can quickly identify mistakes, roll back, and refactor. You're not tied down by your failures.

Me: I see, but these are real users we're talking about...

Doug: There is no better teacher than experience. You must get your product to the users if you ever want to learn anything significant. Will they go through a few hitches? Sure, but that happens with practically every application, right? When you are deploying continuously, when you have that pipeline, you have the power to change it and help that user. Not tomorrow, not next week, now. And that's all that differentiates CD from CD (yes, I know it's confusing). Delivering something constantly and delivering it to the customer are two different things, and one of them is much more valuable than the other.

Me: It makes no sense, but I'll give it a go, sure.

Doug: Do more and you'll learn more.

And so concluded this encounter with Doug. It was insightful but, as always, left me with more questions than answers. He hasn't shown up again since, but I know he's there and will appear when I need him the least, taking me on another mad journey through the *Dougverse...*

That was quite the diatribe ol' DevOps Doug went on, huh? But that is essentially the difference between the two CDs – the philosophical difference between a semi-automatic and an automatic rifle. Each of them has its own uses. One can be seen as an extension of the other, and they both have a place.

Now that we have all of this theorizing out of the way (which is good, because this field is still growing and evolving), we can get to the fun part. Let's do a few tasks that will give us a clearer idea of how to use Python to accomplish these rather ambitious goals. Let's just do a simple one that you can perform with very little setup. Because as someone told me (I can't remember who), "*Do more and you'll learn more.*"

Python CI/CD essentials – automating a basic task

A big yet understated part of DevOps is the thoroughness of the documentation that the process forces you to produce. The documentation does not have to be large; it does not have to be so comprehensive that it confuses people and makes them think twice about ever reading or writing documentation. It must be clear, concise, and to the point. And most of all, it must exist. Seriously, that last part is rarer than you think.

So, how do we use Python to facilitate the documentation process? Well, for this we can use a little library called **Sphinx**. Sphinx is a library written in Python that can be used to generate explicit documentation on a number of code bases, even those not written in Python. Sphinx is one of the most prominent tools for documentation. Most Python frameworks have their documentation written in it. You can install Sphinx through a lot of avenues in all available operating systems, but the one that we are going to use is the classic `pip`:

```
pip install sphinx
```

Once you have done this, go to the root directory of your project and initialize Sphinx using the following command:

```
sphinx-quickstart
```

You'll be given a few settings for the setup. You can leave these as the default for now to get the sample document. You can later change this in the conf.py file.

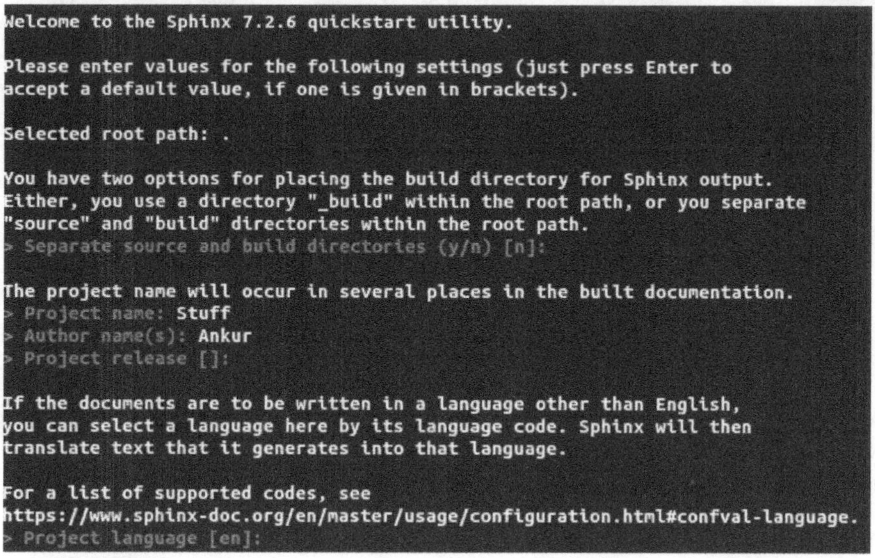

Figure 9.1 – Quickstart menu for Sphinx

This will create an initial directory structure that can be built in HTML or LaTeX, among many other documentation formats.

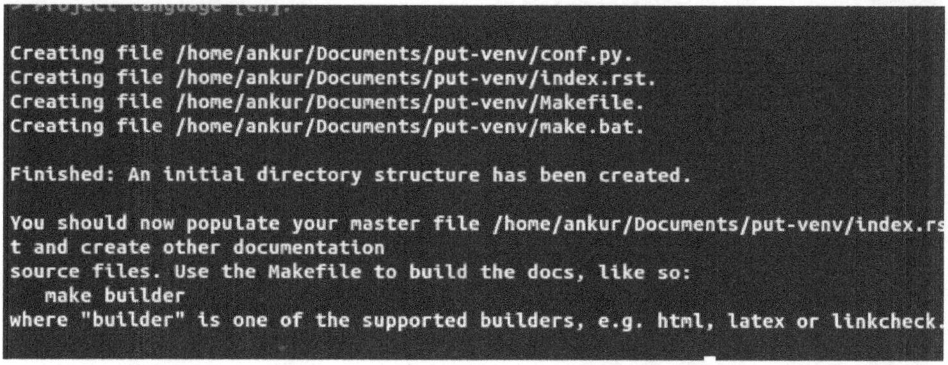

Figure 9.2 – Completion of Sphinx setup

Now, let's write a bit of Python code to use with our Sphinx generator.

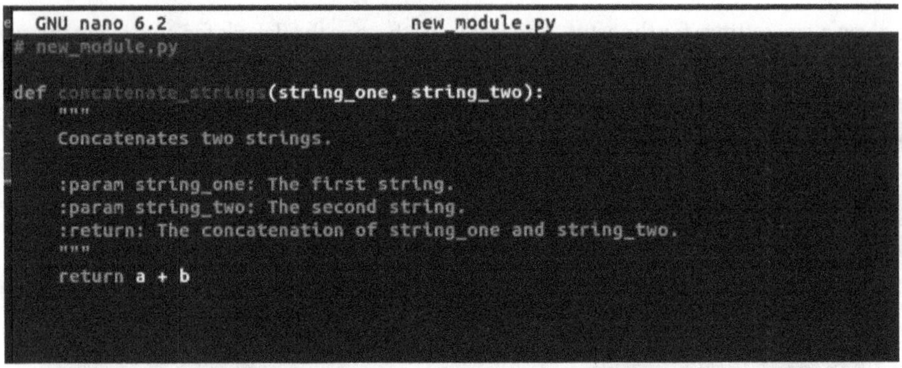

```
GNU nano 6.2                              new_module.py
# new_module.py

def concatenate_strings(string_one, string_two):
    """
    Concatenates two strings.

    :param string_one: The first string.
    :param string_two: The second string.
    :return: The concatenation of string_one and string_two.
    """
    return a + b
```

Figure 9.3 – Initial code to be documented

You'll notice the details in the code comments. These details are what Sphinx references when it creates the documentation. This is why open source projects emphasize code commenting on projects so much. If you ever encounter these comments in libraries, you now know why. Now, run a command to build an HTML file for documentation using the following:

```
make html
```

This will give you a documentation HTML file that you can host that looks something like this:

Stuff

Navigation

Quick search

[   ] Go

Welcome to Stuff's documentation!

Indices and tables

- Index
- Module Index
- Search Page

©2023, Ankur. | Powered by Sphinx 7.2.6 & Alabaster 0.7.13 | Page source

Figure 9.4 – Documentation HTML page

This was, of course, done manually. But with the correct documentation practices, it can be automated with a workflow that runs the preceding commands.

Now, whether you are an experienced DevOps engineer or a novice, you know that one of the main things that a DevOps person has to do (as experienced in this section) is work with developers and ask them to do things that will make the automation process and other DevOps processes smoother. One of the ways to gain a developer's trust in this process is to make their lives easier in some way to prove your worth, and to just be a good co-worker in general. You can do that by being polite, always making a new cup of coffee if it finishes on your pour, holding the door for them… and also, as described in the next section, making their lives a little easier.

Working with devs and infrastructure to deliver your product

Being a DevOps engineer means being the ultimate team player. It also means you have to socialize with and be somewhat liked by practically everyone on your team. And honestly, it's not that hard; laugh at their awkward jokes and make a little small talk and suddenly you're everyone's friend. It's not that hard to get people to work together if you want to. It is, however, quite difficult, some of the time, to get their efforts to coordinate with yours. This is why we have collaboration tools. Besides ordinary GitHub, we have all sorts of tools for whatever development model you are using. Jira, Slack, Zoom, Google Chat, Teams… I could go on forever. What happens quite often is that a lot of teams use multiple collaboration tools. So, the question then becomes, how do we get these collaboration tools to collaborate with each other?

There are a lot of connectors that the tools themselves provide, but sometimes their functionality needs to be facilitated with some code and making a few API calls. We will try this now using Python to connect two very common productivity tools: Todoist and Microsoft To Do. You may have heard about or used either one or both of these tools.

Todoist is a simple to-do list application. There's nothing much to it; it is very similar to other such applications, such as Jira or Trello. Microsoft To Do is the same, except it is integrated into Microsoft 365.

Let's start by extracting a list of tasks from the Todoist API. To do that, let's create a Todoist account and add a few tasks from the UI:

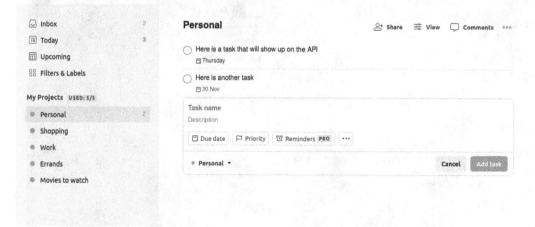

Figure 9.5 – Todoist dashboard

Just a couple of tasks with deadlines there. Now, let's get the API token to call this API. Under your account's **Settings** | **Integrations** | **Developer** tab, you will find the API key, which you can copy and use. Now, you can also install the Python `todoist` library:

```
pip install todoist_api_python
```

Next, write a script that integrates your API token and lists out all the tasks.

```python
from todoist_api_python.api import TodoistAPI
import json

api = TodoistAPI("<your_API_key_here>")

try:
    tasks = api.get_tasks()
    print(json.dumps(tasks,default=lambda o: o.__dict__,
            sort_keys=True, indent=4))
except Exception as error:
    print(error)
```

Figure 9.6 – Code to get Todoist tasks

Simple enough, with a little bit of syntactic sugar, it will get you a list of tasks like this:

```
[
    {
        "assignee_id": null,
        "assigner_id": null,
        "comment_count": 0,
        "content": "Optional report",
        "created_at": "2015-11-21T17:10:52.000000Z",
        "creator_id": "None",
        "description": "",
        "due": {
            "date": "2015-11-22",
            "datetime": null,
            "is_recurring": false,
            "string": "Nov 22",
            "timezone": null
        },
        "id": "1618574692",
        "is_completed": false,
        "labels": [],
        "order": 1,
        "parent_id": null,
        "priority": 1,
        "project_id": "1766864567",
```

Figure 9.7 – Data extracted from the Todoist API

That's just a small sample, but you can see the content, the description, and the due date, which are the things that we are interested in. Now, we are going to attempt to do the same thing with Microsoft To Do. For this, we are simply going to call the API endpoint. There is a library for Microsoft To Do in Python as well, but it is still in the experimental stage.

You will need to get an authorization token from Microsoft, which you can get by calling the API for it, as shown here: `https://learn.microsoft.com/en-us/graph/auth-v2-user?context=graph%2Fapi%2F1.0&view=graph-rest-1.0&tabs=curl`. I'm not including the process for this because it is quite clearly laid out here. You can integrate it into the code later if you want to automatically generate the token. Now, let's modify our code in order to use the content, description, and due date that we have taken from Todoist:

```python
from todoist_api_python.api import TodoistAPI
import json
from datetime import datetime, timezone
import requests
#API tokens
api = TodoistAPI("<your_api_token_here>")
access_token = "<Your_Microsoft_token_here>"
#Endpoint for your default task list
TODO_API_ENDPOINT = YOUR_TODO_ENDPOINThttps://graph.microsoft.com/
v1.0/me/todo/lists/@default/tasks


#Function to create task in Microsoft Todo
def create_todo_task(title,date):
    headers = {'Authorization': 'Bearer '+access_token,
        'Content-Type': 'application/json'}
    payload = {'title': title,
        'dueDateTime': date}
    response = requests.post(TODO_API_ENDPOINT, headers=headers,
json=payload)
    return response.json() if response.status_code == 201 else None
try:
    #Get task in JSON form
    tasks = json.dumps(api.get_tasks(),default=lambda o: o.__
dict__,sort_keys=True, indent=4)
    #Parse tasks
    for task in tasks:
        title = task["content"]
        date = task["due"]["date"].replace(tzinfo=timezone.utc).
astimezone(tz=None)
        #Create tasks based on information
        create_todo_task(title, date)
except Exception as error:
    print(error)
```

And it's as simple as that. We can use this code to take tasks from Todoist and put them in Microsoft To Do. We can even use the **microservices-based architecture** in our previous chapters (like in *Chapter 8, Understanding Event-Driven Architecture*) to make this even more efficient using webhooks and events. Speaking of events, in a lot of servers, one of the most common events is a failure. In the event of a failure, a rollback strategy is needed. Let's see how Python can facilitate that.

Performing rollback

I have said this many times during the course of this book: making mistakes is okay. That is because most mistakes are reversible. Some are not, but those are actually quite easy to recognize if you have your wits about you. In DevOps, this stands true as well. You can reverse your mistakes. Often, the question becomes how quickly, quietly, and effectively you can do this. That is exactly what **rollbacks** do. They aid in the identification and correction of problems.

Rollbacks can be performed manually, or they can be automated. Having a manual rollback at times is too slow and requires people to actually be aware of an incident or an error, something that can take a long time if the team is off on a weekend, for example. In such cases – and in a lot of others – an automatic rollback based on a metric is necessary. And as we all know, Python is good at that stuff.

There are many ways to roll back on a deployment: Blue/Green (50% on the old instance, 50% on the new), canary deployment (a minuscule percentage of users get new features to test them in production), and a whole host of other methods. One of my favorites is the **Red/Black deployment**. In this kind of deployment, there are two instances of an application: the current instance (red) and the future instance (black). You move your endpoint from red to black. If that doesn't work out, you move it back to red. Simple enough, right? Well, here's an illustration, anyway:

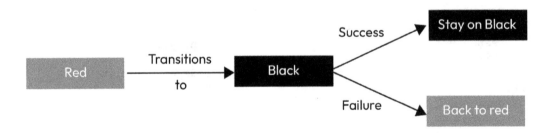

Figure 9.8 – Illustration of red/black deployment

So, remember, *red on black, you're okay Jack, black on red, you're dead.* Oh, no wait, that's coral snakes. But the concept here is simple enough. It's a type of failover that can be handled pretty easily. Most DNS services have this functionality built in. But that doesn't mean it cannot be handled from a coding perspective. The reason we try to handle it like that is to give ourselves a little bit more control and to make room for possible future changes (such as failing over multiple sites at once). So, let's try this from a coding perspective and perform failover using a Lambda microservice on AWS Route 53:

```python
import boto3

def  lambda_handler(event, context):
     domain_name = '<your_domain_name_here>'
    default_endpoint = '<your_endpoint_here>'

    # Initialize the Route 53 client
    client = boto3.client('route53')

    # Get the hosted zone ID for the domain
    response = client.list_hosted_zones_by_name(DNSName=domain_name)
    hosted_zone_id = response['HostedZoneId']

    # Update the Route 53 record set to point to the default endpoint
    changes= {
        'Changes': [
            {
                'Action': 'UPSERT',
                'ResourceRecordSet': {
                    'Name': domain_name,
                    'Type': 'A',
                    'TTL': 300,
                    'ResourceRecords': [{'Value': default_endpoint}]
                }
            }
        ]
    }

    client.change_resource_record_sets(
     HostedZoneId=hosted_zone_id,
     ChangeBatch=changes
)

    return {
    'statusCode': 200,
    'body': "Nothing, really, no one's gonna see this}"
    }
```

Well, that's the code. Stick it in a Lambda function and have the proper conditions to trigger that Lambda function and you can reset back to a set default whenever you want. Of course, you can do this with regular Route 53 as well, but this gives a whole host of options for modifications. Modifications are a very important part of the CI/CD process, where nothing is solid forever.

Summary

So, let's summarize what you've learned in this chapter. You have learned that the philosophy and methodology of DevOps is an ever-flowing river, constantly in flux. You have also learned that you must adopt a similar philosophy while working with CI/CD. In the next section, you learned about a basic CI/CD task that can be performed in Python. We followed this up with the next section, where you learned how to help out your developers by making their day-to-day tasks easier and making sure that they have all the convenience and productivity tools they need. This was followed up with a lesson on performing rollbacks and a rather unique technique for a simple rollback.

If you have tolerated all of that, thank you. You're nine chapters into this book and I still somehow have your attention. I must be doing something well, right? Maybe? Well, let's look ahead to the next chapter – the next section, actually – because we're about to get even more ambitious with our ideas. We are going to look at how some large companies use Python in their everyday work. Sounds exciting!

Part 3: Let's Go Further, Let's Build Bigger

In this part, we will take our DevOps and Python skills and knowledge to the next level and look at some advanced concepts regarding the subject.

This part has the following chapters:

10

Common DevOps Use Cases in Some of the Biggest Companies in the World

I take great satisfaction in seeing people and organizations achieve goals they might have originally believed to be beyond their reach.

– Don W. Wilson

Throughout this book, I have asked you to have a lot of faith in me and the things that I write. I have asked you to have an even greater amount of faith in the process of **DevOps** and the fruits that it will eventually yield. With the start of this new section, I suppose it is time for me to put my money where my mouth is and show you a few things under the hood.

All of this chapter is based on public information either provided by the company that implemented the use case or the company that consulted on it. They can be found publicly in each of the major cloud companies' customer success story pages. This business information has been willingly put out there in order to serve as an example of how other businesses and people in the industry can make their own workloads better.

I'm going to use these use cases as an example of what you can do with DevOps and how you can support their use using Python. I didn't want to use hypotheticals for this part because that would have been disingenuous. However, the way I have used these cases is meant to represent how they can be replicated using Python as opposed to whether they have used Python or not. They may have, but that's not pertinent.

The primary motivation behind this chapter is to show you that there are real places where the philosophies of DevOps have been used in order to create genuine value for customers. This is a justification of the skills that you have been learning during your DevOps journey and during the course of this book.

So, without further ado, in this chapter, you will learn about the following:

- An **Amazon Web Services** (**AWS**) use case that helped bridge the divide between business analysts and data engineers

- An Azure use case that saved a lot of coding time and helped make deployments more efficient

- Two **Google Cloud Platform** (**GCP**) use cases involving sports leagues finding solutions that made their league more accessible

AWS use case – Samsung electronics

Samsung uses cloud and DevOps principles for a lot of stuff. That's pretty obvious since Samsung is massive. It is why I haven't given them a proper introduction, because, well, you know what Samsung is. The particular case that we will be talking about is an interesting one: one that involves getting the layman business analyst involved in **machine learning** (**ML**) while also allowing the people who know how to write ML algorithms and applications in code to have their abilities maximized. It is a two-pronged approach playing to the abilities of both, enhancing the feedback from both of them and increasing collaboration between them. The following figure shows Samsung's original workflow for data analytics:

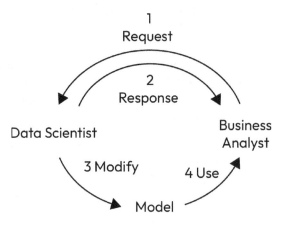

Figure 10.1 – Samsung's original workflow for data analytics

So, let's break down the scenario that Samsung was confronted with and the methods that they used to resolve it.

Scenario

Samsung's analytical team consisted of two different sections: business analysts and data scientists. The business analysts looked at the problem and data provided by Samsung's consumer electronics from the perspective of people who could understand human behavior and how it could be used to improve products and predict customer behavior.

To do this, they required data, lots of data, and the ability to process it. This is where the data scientists came in; they turned the hunches that the analysts had into cases that could be solved to provide concrete data. They created data analytics and ML algorithms to provide insights that the business analysts would use to provide recommendations and advice on how to continue with their products. They would also provide feedback to the data science team.

However, this partnership was not as smooth as one would believe; there was a gap between the two teams because of a number of factors, the primary factor being that there was a disparity between how the two teams did their jobs despite being dependent on each other.

In addition to that, data scientists had to do repetitive tasks on different datasets in order to ensure that the correct output was being given back to the business analysts. This resulted in the data scientists not having the time to experiment with other ML algorithms and various techniques that they might have wanted to implement. It also resulted in the business analysts having significantly less control over the data that they were responsible for, meaning that they didn't have the full picture to make an effective analysis.

The need became to find a way to coordinate the data and the algorithms in such a way that the more common algorithms could be used by the business analysts while being tweaked by the data scientists at the same time. This would create an environment where the data scientists did not have to wait on the business analysts and vice versa, freeing up time and resources for both.

Brainstorming

Now, you may ask, if you are unfamiliar with the process, in the modern world, what is a business analyst doing if they don't know how to write code? Well, that's a lot more common than you think. An analyst's job is not to write code or parse through data (though this can often be something they do); their job is to analyze the information put in front of them and use that to provide some sort of recommendation, insight, or solution.

The crux of the problem here is the fact that there is a gap in communication and understanding between the two teams concerned that is quite difficult to bridge without major personnel upheaval. And that kind of upheaval is usually not in the best interests of the company.

You need to make it so that one team is not dependent upon the other and can operate on the information that they receive as opposed to the people that they receive it from (loosely coupled, remember?). So, an ideal solution would be to find a way to allow both teams to work on the same data at the same time without hindering each other through unnecessary communication, and that is exactly the solution that they found.

Solution

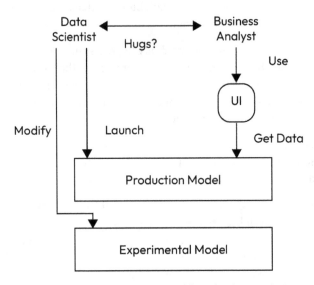

Figure 10.2 – Samsung's new workflow for data analytics

The solution was essentially this: there would be a single source of data that both the analysts and the data scientists could work from; the data scientists would give the analysts access to a user interface from which they could perform the data operations that they wanted. The scientists would then tweak those operations and algorithms, trying to get better results without the analysts having to contact them to get results on the version of the algorithm that was currently running. This was essentially like creating an application for internal use for data analysts that was built by the data scientists.

Different skills and mindsets exist for a reason, and this is why there needs to be different people with varied roles and perspectives on a team. The only thing to do in such a scenario is to ensure that all of these roles are put in a position to succeed. By giving both these roles a platform and a workflow in which they would be comfortable, a reasonable way was found for the whole team to work optimally. Samsung did this by making the data centralized, with both teams having access to it and with neither team needing to be dependent on the other to make forward progress, and yet at the same time finding a way in which they could complement and support each other.

Next, we will look at a use case where the company had to deal with managing people who have similar skill sets with varying levels of experience, while also juggling business needs and productivity.

Azure Use Case – Intertech

While searching through use cases and scenarios, I absolutely fell in love with what Intertech did through the power of DevOps transformation. The fact that it used Azure is not as relevant as what it did with Azure and how it used the Azure and GitHub services to modernize and revolutionize its pipelines. This use case is all that DevOps is supposed to bring to a company in terms of value. It also addresses something that will become very relevant in the later parts of this book (where we are now): generative AI. Let's take a look at the old Intertech workflow:

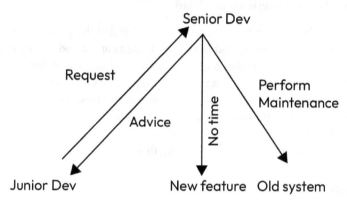

Figure 10.3 – Old Intertech workflow

This figure represents a sort of sunk cost fallacy, one that can lead to a severe loss of productivity. It represents how Intertech operated suboptimally and wasted much of their critical personnel in tasks that should have not been their concern in the first place. So, let's look at how Intertech approaches this problem.

Let's start with who Intertech are. They are an IT operations company that supports some of the largest business clients in Turkey with their infrastructure and operational needs. Now, you can imagine that this kind of operation would be pretty difficult to manage on a lot of levels. The pains are not very big; in fact, they are tiny cuts and pinpricks, but those are often the most annoying kinds of pain. They are irritating and distracting, and if you let them, they will steal your attention. In this section, we will talk about mental and physical anguish and how the fine people at Intertech worked to reduce it.

Scenario

Intertech worked in creating and maintaining solutions for some of the biggest companies in Turkey. Make a mental note of those two words: creating and maintaining. Those are two of the fundamental parts of developing any software solution, but they are very different from each other. To create something is to give it life; you're giving birth, it's painful, and it's long, but it's wonderful. Maintaining something is changing the diapers on the thing you gave birth to. It's disgusting, but you are responsible for it and the toddler isn't just going to take care of itself, no matter how prepared or independent it may be (and most toddlers are not). Keep this analogy in mind as it'll follow us throughout the subsections. Years down the line, if I'm changing the diapers on this book to write a second edition, I will keep this in mind as well.

So, this was the difficulty facing Intertech: the balance of developing new projects while maintaining old ones. And the tasks to maintain the old ones were mundane, but they required man-hours, manpower, and a lot of power hours that could've been spent coming up with new ways to deliver value. The cycle of thought that runs between the initial problem and finally finding its solution requires precious time and intellectual effort that is usually significantly less than the capacity of the person solving it. Basically, it forces intelligent people to do dumb tasks.

So, when thinking about the solution to this, what should be the first thing we think of? Perhaps there is a way in which solutions can be found without having to think about and research them too much. Not, of course, for critical, vital tasks that require actual focus but for mundane tasks that require several Googles of a bunch of terms to get to the appropriate Stack Overflow page and then copying and pasting that into a solution and running it a couple of times to make sure it works. Maybe there's a tool that will collate all of this information and generate a simple concise solution for a simple mundane problem and save us all some time. Perhaps one that rhymes with *hartificial fintelligence*? Alright, nothing rhymes with artificial intelligence. AI, that's what I'm talking about.

Brainstorming

Well, by now, you probably know where this is heading, so let me share my personal experience on how I usually use generative AI in my daily life. It is a useful tool, as most of you who read this book will attest to unless you are staunchly against AI or have all the information in the world stored in your head. If you have the latter, contact me and tell me what actually happened with *The Sopranos* ending.

I use generative AI to lay down the steps towards a solution and frame it in a way that I can understand and modify according to the context I may have given, or ones which it hasn't been trained on yet. This is so much easier than having to look at a tutorial whenever I have to find a way to fix something, and then when that tutorial is incomplete, having to find another one. With generative AIs such as ChatGPT, the tables are turned; it is my prerogative now to be impatient and that of the generative AI to be persistent and patient with my requests. This is amazing because, honestly, thinking is exhausting, especially if you have to think about the same thing over and over again. It makes your mind go numb, and it reduces your productivity. The people of Intertech came to the same conclusion.

If you want to follow along with the child analogy, this is like having a magical force that will change the diaper and wrap it around the child just waiting for you to put the pin on it. So, in that vein, if there is a repetitive task that comes in and is simple enough, it can hamper productivity through all of these ways. In such cases, it is generative AI that can come to the rescue. Any of you who have ever used it know how useful ChatGPT is at this. In fact, in my personal experience, the most useful thing that ChatGPT does for me is explaining lines of code that I paste into it. It would take me more than the several seconds that it takes ChatGPT to do it because I simply cannot collect the information as fast as the AI can. So, now that we have justified our generative AI solution, let's see how Intertech –

who came to a similar conclusion – used these concepts and integrated them into their DevOps and Azure workloads and tasks.

Solution

The solution that was created by Intertech revolved around the use of GitHub Copilot and Azure's OpenAI integration. Copilot, once trained on the code for a particular repository that was in need of maintenance, could simply write the required scripts if given the correct prompts. Intertech integrated Copilot into the **integrated development environments (IDEs)** used by their developers so that once they wrote a line or two, Copilot simply inferred what their intentions were and wrote much of the rest. The developers simply had to verify a couple of tests and voilà, an efficient code delivery system, one that frees up time and thinking power. The following figure demonstrates the solution:

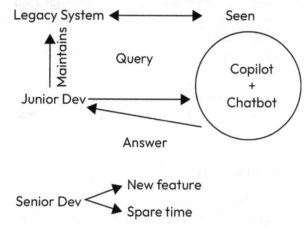

Figure 10.4 – New Intertech workflow with generative AI

The solution in the diagram can be broken down into the following steps:

1. When a junior developer performs maintenance on a legacy system, they use an instance of Copilot which has been trained on the system's code base.

2. This allows them to query and find the answers about the code base that they are looking for in a human-readable form.

3. Copilot also helps autocomplete their code in the style of the rest of the code base, maintaining consistency.

4. The senior developer is, for the most part, removed from this process, allowing them to work on newer projects and systems.

Since most of the maintenance operations were being done on the time of the senior developers as they had worked on the older projects, these developers (whose time is more precious because of their depth of experience) were the ones who needed to get hands-on with a lot of the issues to solve them. Even when these issues were handed off to junior developers, they still asked the senior developers for a large amount of advice, which while not negative behavior at all, still hindered the senior developers to an extent.

To make the junior developers less reliant on seniors for advice on the code base, the company integrated Azure OpenAI chatbots into their IDEs. These chatbots could scrape and infer information from the code and the documentation for projects and answer questions about them to the satisfaction of the junior developers most of the time. This reduced the amount of time taken by senior personnel in maintaining the code and it guided the junior developers through the code base using their very own personalized babysitter, if you will. One incredible consequence of this was that the number of emails sent within the company was reduced by 50%, which is a remarkable number. Wouldn't you like 50% fewer emails for the same if not greater amount of productivity? Not to mention all of the time that is freed up by not being in meetings and having to retread old stuff. This is the kind of value multiplier that can take companies to the next level.

Speaking of value, so far the value that we have seen has been values on fact sheets and computer code, but in our next section, we will see the value that DevOps can generate in a more physically tangible environment using sports as an example.

Google Cloud use case – MLB and AFL

If there is one thing that you should know about me, it is that I am a massive sports fan. I am, and I love learning about new sports just as much as following the old ones that I have followed for years.

I have been following **Major League Baseball** (**MLB**) for years, and in those years, baseball has always been the sport of analytics. Most modern teams in their team selection are driven by analytics and the performance of players is measured through statistical analysis of a number of metrics that are collected when they play their games. You may have seen the film *Moneyball* (or read the book by Michael Lewis), which chronicles the introduction of statistical methods in the choice of baseball players and how they led to the success of the Oakland Athletics baseball team in the late 90s and early 2000s.

In the MLB, one of the results of the introduction of analytical data is the analysis of the gameplay itself and the time taken to finish a game. In order to streamline the game, MLB introduced the pitch clock, giving players only 15 seconds to throw a pitch. The clock, as seen in the following figure, needs to synchronize throughout the arena and with the clock that is being broadcast over television as well. This synchronization presents a unique challenge for MLB to implement its newest rule:

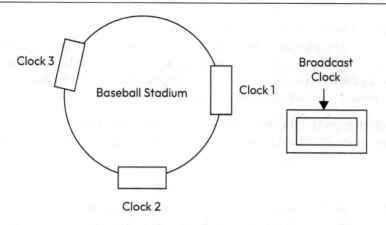

Figure 10.5 – Original MLB play clock system

I wanted to also look at some other sports leagues that may have used data analytics and Google Cloud in some way and integrated it into their league's infrastructure (perhaps in a way that was different from MLB's approach). In my search, I found the perfect example with the **Australian Football League** (**AFL**). The following diagram shows the AFL's broadcast situation for coaching:

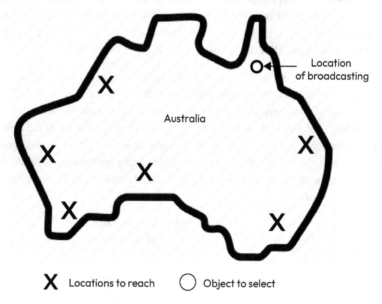

Figure 10.6 – The AFL broadcast situation for coaching

When I started this, I knew practically nothing about Australian rules football (also known as Aussie rules football) or the AFL other than the fact that the day of the Grand Final is a public holiday in Australia. However, one thing that I did figure out during my research was that both of these companies were using advanced analytics in order to find ways to improve the way that the play was seen and to analyze if there was a way to make the gameplay and the players even better.

Given my passion for sports and all the nerd stuff surrounding sports, this little section now seems inevitable to me. So, let's dive in and see what DevOps and data insights we can find in these use cases.

Scenario

Let's start with baseball; I love baseball. It is the sport of the stoic man; it is the sport where time stands still. If you ever have 23 hours to spare, do yourself a favor and watch Ken Burns' *Baseball* documentary series; you will not regret it. But baseball as a whole and MLB in particular suffered from a few setbacks the past few years. There was a cheating scandal involving the Houston Astros and live attendance and viewership were down because of the excessive length of the games. To solve these problems while maintaining the integrity of the game, MLB turned to data. They turned to the analytics that the teams individually used and decided to turn it toward the league as a whole. They collected statistics related to gameplay, attendance, and viewer engagement from all of the available games throughout the season (2,430 games plus playoffs) and decided to create infrastructure solutions to bolster the solutions that they would implement. They used Google Cloud for this: both for the data analytics and the implementation of the solution itself.

Aussie rules football is the number one sport in Australia. In the land down under, it is the sport that has the greatest viewership and the biggest audience. It is also the most physical sport played in Australia and as someone who watches a lot of sports and does a lot of data science, the more physical a sport is in terms of physical contact between human beings, the more difficult it becomes to analyze that sport. Here, the data needs to be broken down on a more physical level, looking toward the human body itself. This approach allowed the AFL to develop a system that used ML with human coaching to develop systems of training for the underprivileged and differently able people who were still passionate about the sport.

Two very different problems were faced by these two sports leagues, both of which required completely different approaches, but both of which were solved in Google Cloud using the principles of DevOps. Let's see how they did it.

Brainstorming

MLB problem was one that affected the game and people's enjoyment of it. People hate it when you waste their time, and they hate slow games. Anyone who has ever watched the last two minutes of a close NBA playoff game knows. MLB approached this problem by looking at the time taken every inning and what were the longest aspects of those innings. They realized that pickoffs and the time taken by pitchers to wind up their pitch were slowing down the game. This led to the creation of the pitch clock, a timer for how long a pitcher can wait between pitches thrown. They had determined that this time between pitches was the main reason that the game had slowed down and they believed that the clock would rectify the situation. It was implemented using GCP and DevOps principles combining the GCP services with on-premises timing hardware. And as a fan, I am very grateful for it as well. We will discuss the full extent of the solution in the next section.

The problem with the AFL was one of youth outreach and the physical limitations that some people have when attempting to play the sport. Australia is also a massive country with a very widespread populace, meaning that people in rural areas who needed training in Aussie rules football would need to have their training and coaching administered remotely. The goal then became to reach as many people as possible and to do so with as much data as possible so that it would be accurate, and also to reach people who are impaired in some form of communication. This problem required an approach of communication between devices as well as the use of ML algorithms, particularly for use in tracking the ball used in the sport with respect to the player who is being coached.

So, looking at these problems, and the approaches we could potentially take to solve them, we can now start coming up with a couple of solutions that might help these organizations achieve their goals. Let's see what exactly it was that they did to achieve these goals.

Solution

The solution to MLB's problems involved using Google Cloud's Anthos service mesh to coordinate all the pitch clocks together. Centralized yet distributed time clocks added to the integrity of the game and these new rules.

The problem with MLB was one of synchronization. The goal was to synchronize the play clocks that were running throughout the stadium, to coordinate their timing. Here, Google used their Anthos service mesh (as shown in the following diagram) as a sort of connector between a number of devices in the cloud and on-premises devices at baseball stadiums. This allowed the timer for pitchers to be visible and accurate everywhere with no delays, ensuring the fairness of the new system.

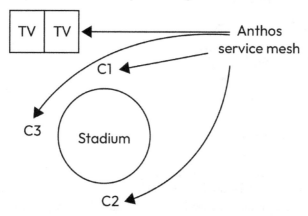

Figure 10.7 – Anthos synchronized game clock for MLB

The introduction of the play clock reduced the time of games for the average baseball game by 24 minutes. That is significant and I think it is the most significant application of the DevOps philosophy that I have seen in such a non-tech scenario. Let's do the math here: 24 minutes was reduced from every game, which increased the average attendance of games from 26,843 to 29,295, which is a significant achievement. So, how much time was really saved? Well, that is 24 minutes x 29,295 people x 2,430 regular season games. That is 1,708,484,400 minutes in total saved, which is 28,474,740 hours, 1,186,447.5 days, or 3,250 years. That is quite the saving, and the fans have felt it too, which is why the attendance is up. All of this is because of the ability to coordinate loosely coupled infrastructure.

The approach to the AFL's problem required the delivery of ML models that could perform motion tracking over networks that were not always reliable. This meant that any sort of ML model that was used would have to use the computing power on the side of the mobile device and be lightweight enough to not affect the functioning of that device. Google's development team had helped facilitate a similar teaching solution with cricket in the **Indian Premier League** (**IPL**). So, the solution that they ended up with was an application called the Footy Skills app.

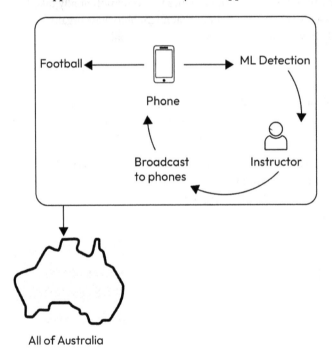

Figure 10.8 – Instruction broadcast system for AFL coaching

The application used two ML models: one to detect an Aussie rules ball based on size, shape, and color, and another to determine its spatial depth and location. They also added features that would assist the hearing and visually impaired as well as wheelchair-using athletes who played the sport.

Summary

This chapter was quite the journey. It was unique, even among some of the weird stuff I have written in this book. But I can honestly say that it was an enjoyable chapter to write simply because of all of the unique solutions that I got to research while I was writing it.

We started with the AWS solution and that was a great demonstration of what can happen when you put people in a position where their skills can be valued and used with other skills as opposed to clashing with them. It also showed us how DevOps solutions don't just facilitate technologies, but the people behind those technologies as well.

In the Azure use case, we learned about how AI and ML mixed with DevOps can increase the productivity of a team that engages in creative endeavors. We saw how generative AI is being used to facilitate developers, reduce the amount of mundane and redundant work that key personnel have to do, and free up time and communication channels to make teams more productive.

In the first GCP use case, MLB needed a way to justify changing rules in baseball that had been around for over a century. They used solid data and hard facts to do this. These facts were provided through the collation of data from an entire season of baseball. They then used this and other loosely coupled coordination technology to implement their vision of changed rules. Through data and technological coordination, they achieved the creation of a rule that was profitable to them but also popular with the fans: a feat that is practically unheard of.

In the second GCP use case, the AFL extended its range of availability and inclusivity using ML models delivered with DevOps principles directly onto devices that were spread throughout Australia, giving people in even the most remote areas of Australia access to great coaching and instruction to help them improve in the sport. This gave the AFL an invaluable platform for growth and outreach amongst their fans and future players.

So, in conclusion, this DevOps stuff is pretty useful in real life. A lot of these solutions couldn't have been done without Python either, especially the ones that involved ML and AI. And that is just the beginning of how high you can go with DevOps. In the next chapter, we will dive even deeper into the data science aspect of DevOps, Python with data, and **MLOps**.

11

MLOps and DataOps

The future will soon be a thing of the past.

– George Carlin

I was going to use a bit of generative AI to write the content of this chapter but that would make it more of an autobiography than a technical book, since then the generative AI would become a co-author. I will try to be a very objective observer and do some justice to this hot topic. I hope this will give me a favorable position in a possible future ruled by AI. There are many reasons why there has been such great progress in the field of machine learning and AI in the past century: Noam Chomsky, Alan Turing, the creation of computers themselves, science fiction novels, and man's eternal longing for new life in the universe. But in the past few years, the delivery of these concepts as viable products and services has required the DevOps touch. After all, how else do you think **ChatGPT** manages to instantly answer your four-paragraph questions in about five seconds and does it for a million more people every minute?

Now, all of the chapters and concepts in this book have gotten us back to one fact, which is that DevOps is about delivering value and making things work. And that is no different when the focus of DevOps is data. In such cases, Python becomes even more useful because it is the language of the data operator. Most people and development environments for data usually default to Python these days because of the existence of the necessary tools for data processing and analysis. Most effective **DataOps** workloads will use Python in some capacity. A lot of them will use Python both on the running script as well as any supporting operational scripts that they may need to write. We will also talk about **MLOps** and the operations that help deliver and optimize machine learning models and algorithms. We will talk about all of this and more in this chapter after you have read through the *Technical requirements* section.

To summarize, in this chapter, you will learn the following:

- The difference in the approach taken when DataOps/MLOps is in play as opposed to regular DevOps
- The approaches to deal with a variety of different data-based challenges
- The Ops behind the delivery of ChatGPT to your computer screen

Technical requirements

Here are some requirements that will help you follow along with this chapter's activities:

- A GitHub account and access to this book's Git repository (`https://github.com/PacktPublishing/Hands-On-Python-for-DevOps`)

- A Google account to use Google Colab

- A usable Python environment somewhere

- A nice cup of your favorite beverage

How MLOps and DataOps differ from regular DevOps

A question that we often encounter in any sort of technical industry in general is: what is the difference between a data role and a non-data role? What would be the difference between a software and data engineer, a data analyst and an accountant, or a DJ and a music composer? It is something employers ask a lot; people speculate on whether one is a subgroup of another or whether they are completely different. Even in the Swedish language, *dator* means "computer," science is translated as *vetenskap*, and computer science is referred to as *datavetenskap*, so at some point whatever entity that designs and updates the Swedish language thought that there was very little to distinguish between the two.

We will now explain this through a couple of common DevOps use cases that can be applied and used in these more narrowed fields of DataOps and MLOps. For DataOps, we will go through a method that is simple but has saved me a lot of data concatenation operations in Python when using JSON files. For MLOps, we will focus on the GPU side, which is the primary hardware that an MLOps engineer may have to work with.

DataOps use case – JSON concatenation

This is quite a simple little trick, but one that is not as commonly known as you think. I honestly think if I can help even one person working with data with this section, I will have succeeded. The manipulation of JSON is a very important aspect of data operations that is very prominent, especially in NoSQL use cases, but also in a number of other cases. The ability to naturally manipulate JSON gives Python a major advantage over a lot of other programming languages. One of the most useful applications of this is the pipe (|) operator. This little operator can be used to perform concatenations, unions, and even bitwise operations on numbers. It is one of the many ways in which Python has made it easier to perform these small data operations for ease of use.

So, we will begin with just the function for the concatenation of one JSON with another:

```
a = {"one":1, "two":2}
b = {"one":"one", "two":2, "three":3}

print(a|b)
```

That's it. That's the code, and here's the output of that code:

```
{'one': 'one', 'two': 2, 'three': 3}
```

Figure 11.1 – Output of JSON concatenation

You'll see that the second JSON's value for a key overrides the value from the first JSON and that if they have the same common values, they will stay the same, and any additional values are combined into the overall JSON. So, with all that in mind, whenever you encounter such a problem with JSON combination (and it can come up quite often), you will have this little trick in your toolbelt. Now, let's move on to another trick, one that will certainly help all you gaming hardware addicts out there. It'll help the rest of you out too, but I like mentioning hardware addicts because they make the most YouTube videos and I'm hoping to get some of that sweet exposure.

MLOps use case – overclocking a GPU

In this modern age of AI art, image generation at the highest levels can require a lot of processing power. For any kind of graphical rendering, CPUs are only used when no other options are available and are usually not recommended for larger renderings. For machine learning TensorFlow algorithms, Google's proprietary TPUs are the norm. But again, for anything concerning image generation or manipulation, a good GPU is good to have. And if the rare case comes up where that GPU needs a bit of extra juice to get things done, overclocking can be necessary.

A lot of the time, GPU processors have their own drivers and with their drivers come their own command-line tools. Executing these before and after the use of overclocking or another GPU feature can be a hassle. Instead, using Python's in-built subprocess module, we can automatically overclock or perform any other GPU processes that we would like. For this example, we are going to use the CLI tools for NVIDIA, which is probably the most popular GPU brand available at the moment. NVIDIA has a command-line tool called **nvidia-smi**, which also contains an overclocking feature and is what we are going to invoke. Now, let's write the code block that will help us overclock our GPUs:

```
import subprocess

def overclock_gpu():
    # Set the new clock frequency for memory and graphics
    new_clock_memory= <your_clock_frequency_in_MHz>
    new_clock_graphics= <your_clock_frequency_in_MHz>

    # Run NVIDIA command to overclock GPU
    command = "nvidia-smi -i 0 --applications-clocks {new_clock_
memory},{new_clock_graphics}"
    subprocess.run(command, shell=True)
```

```
if __name__ == "__main__":
    overclock_gpu()
```

The preceding code, when run, will overclock whichever NVIDIA GPU has been set up on your device. This, in turn, will make processes such as image processing and generation faster. This can be useful when there is a higher demand for these resources, and it isn't possible to shift those demands to other resources. So, this code can be used to temporarily overclock a GPU based on some condition that may cause it to be called. Once it has been overclocked, you can set it back to its default by running the following command (in or out of script):

```
nvidia-smi -- reset-applications-clocks
```

So, this is how you would manipulate GPUs using Python. A lot of this section has involved learning how to manipulate data and the aspects surrounding data. However, the data itself can be difficult to work with for a variety of other reasons as well. One of the primary reasons can be just how much data is there, which can be a lot. The next section will be all about finding ways to not be overwhelmed by all of the data that comes from various sources that you may have to deal with.

Dealing with velocity, volume, and variety

When given any tutorial on how to process data, you are usually given a quick introduction to the **three Vs** (**velocity**, **volume**, and **variety**). These are the three ways in which the complexity of data can scale. Each of them presents a singularly unique problem when dealing with data, and a lot of data that you would have to deal with can be a combination of all three. Velocity is the speed of data coming in over a period of time, volume is the amount of data, and variety is the diversity of the data being presented.

So, this section will be divided according to the three Vs, and in each subsection, there will be a solution for a common problem that may arise with them. This way, you will get to see how Python can help in dealing with such massive amounts of data. Let's start with volume as it is the simplest and probably the first thing that comes to people's minds when it comes to **big data**.

Volume

The volume of data is a pretty simple thing. It represents a certain quantity of data, most, if not all, of which will be of the same type. If we are going to deal with a large volume of data, it will require understanding the time sensitivity of data as well as the resources that we would have on hand. The volume of data that is usually processed differs based on whether the data is massive based on width or length (i.e., whether there are a lot of fields for one row of data or there is a massive number of data rows). Both of these require different solutions, even specialized databases sometimes. There is also the possibility of datasets not being numbers and letters at all but instead being files of audio or video. In this section, we will use an example that will be very useful when we have a database or data file that contains a large number of fields/columns.

To start, we will need a high-volume dataset, so we will use an app called **Mockaroo**, which allows you to generate data fields and sample data using generative AI (very fitting in this chapter). Let's go to the Mockaroo site and generate a few fields for our sample data:

Figure 11.2 – Mockaroo schema

The dataset we produced with Mockaroo looks like the following:

Figure 11.3 – Sample CSV created by Mockaroo

The preceding figure shows just a small piece of it; it's 20 very large fields for 1,000 rows. Let's write the script to parse through it:

```python
import csv

def read_large_csv(file_path):
    with open(file_path, 'r') as csv_file:
        csv_reader = csv.reader(csv_file)
        next(csv_reader, None)
        for row in csv_reader:
            yield row
```

```
csv_file_path = 'MOCK_DATA.csv'
for row in read_large_csv(csv_file_path):
    print(row)
```

The script may seem a little redundant in terms of reading the CSV file, but the reason it is like this is so that all of the rows in the CSV aren't loaded into the memory of the OS at the same time. This method will reduce the load on the memory of the data and is a great way to read large amounts of data in a system where the memory can't hold a lot of data. What it does is that it reads one row of the data and then releases that data from the memory before reading the other rows. This is efficient management of memory during the reading of a high volume of data, which in turn makes the reading a lot faster and smoother, as demonstrated in this diagram:

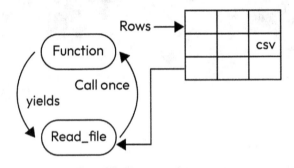

Figure 11.4 – Workflow behind a generator

Now, that was simple enough, but what happens when it's just one row at a time, but constant, such as streaming data? All of it needs to be processed live as it comes in. How would we achieve this? Let's find out.

Velocity

Tackling the velocity of data is a legitimate billion-dollar question. Even today, the biggest video streamers struggle to send out livestream data consistently. Of course, there are a number of reasons for this, but the fact is a lot of solutions don't have the right combination of budget and quality to be consistent all of the time. We can get pretty close, though.

In this exercise, we will be using something that a lot of people call the future, and perhaps the present, of data streaming: **Apache Flink**. This is a stream and batch processing framework developed by the Apache Software Foundation for a smooth, fast data flow. Unlike a lot of frameworks managed by the Apache Software Foundation, this one was created with the express intent of being maintained by them as opposed to a project created by a company and made open source for easier maintenance.

Flink itself does not offer any data storage solutions and is instead simply supposed to process incoming data into a storage location. It has APIs in Java, Python, and Scala, and support on all cloud platforms.

To start with Python, you will need to install `pyflink` using the following command:

```
pip install apache-flink
```

Also install pandas if you have not:

```
pip install pandas
```

Alright, now let's write some code to stream data from a bunch of JSON rows to a CSV table. This is just a sample program to show Flink's workflow, but it does serve that purpose rather effectively:

```python
from pyflink.common import Row
from pyflink.datastream import StreamExecutionEnvironment
from pyflink.table import StreamTableEnvironment, DataTypes
from pyflink.table.descriptors import FileSystem, Json, Schema
import pandas as pd

#Function to use
def flink_input(input_data):
    # Set up the Flink environment
    env = StreamExecutionEnvironment.get_execution_environment()
    t_env = StreamTableEnvironment.create(env)

    # Define the CSV file to output to along with temporary table name
    t_env.connect(FileSystem().path('output.csv')) \
        .with_format(Json().fail_on_missing_field(True)) \
        .with_schema(Schema().field('data', DataTypes.STRING())) \
        .create_temporary_table('output_table')

    # Convert multiple JSON values into PyFlink CSV rows
    input_rows = [Row(json.dumps(json_obj)) for json_obj in input_data]
    df = pd.DataFrame([r[0] for r in input_rows], columns=['data'])

    # Insert the rows into the output table which in turn inserts them
into the CSV file
    t_env.from_pandas(df).insert_into('output_table')

    # Execute the Flink job
    env.execute('CSVJob')
```

```
input_data = [{'key1': 'value1'}, {'key2': 'value2'}, {'key3':
'value3'}]
flink_input(input_data)
```

In this code, you'll see that the JSON rows are inserted into a CSV using a temporary table as a holdover for insertion. This temporary table, when inserted, also inserts the data into the CSV file.

This is a rather simple explanation of the capabilities of Flink, whose job is to work with essentially the same context, but for millions of bits of streaming data at the same time. So, a scaled-up version of the code looks similar, and essentially performs the same function, except it would perform those operations on a larger amount of data. There are a lot of other operations that Flink can perform, an absolute vast quantity (one of the reasons it is so popular), and they all follow a similar pattern and can be integrated with most available data sources.

Now, we will move on to deal with a complication in data that is far too often experienced, and indeed one that always needs to be dealt with in some form. The next section is about variety.

Variety

Variety is interesting and is probably the most complicated burden that most people who work with data deal with. Data can come in all shapes and sizes and often comes in the most expected ways. Many hackers attempt SQL injection attacks by adding valid SQL queries as form fields, which can then cause those queries to run if the data input matches properly. A good quality assurance tester always attempts a variety of tests that try to befuddle a lot of applications by using data types that they should not be able to input into certain fields. But often – when just regular people are given access to a keyboard – what happens is that people will find some way to break a lot of the safety measures placed in a system by pure accident, showing previously unknown system bugs or vulnerabilities.

So, now we are going to go into an example where such a thing can happen, and this is especially prominent in a lot of looser NoSQL databases that may not have all of the standard data formatting built into them. We are going to attempt to insert emojis into a JSON file. Emojis are usually covered under the UTF-8 format, but this format, while readily available on web pages, usually needs to be set on most databases for when more unconventional formats are used.

We will be using Google Colab for this exercise because it is more efficient for something that is a concise proof of concept such as this. Let's start by adding a JSON variable containing an emoji:

```
user_data = {
'username': 'user_with_emoji😊',
}
```

Now, we are going to insert it into a file, first without any UTF-8 formatting:

```
import json

with open('sample.json', 'w') as file:
json.dump(user_data, file)
```

This produces sample JSON with the format shown here:

Figure 11.5 – Storage of emoji without UTF-8 format

This JSON, when converted back for a web page, will require an extra parsing step that may slow down the web page. So, in order to avoid that, we can find a way to store the emoji in the way that it was input. The final output of the code will look more correct, like the following:

Figure 11.6 – Storage of emoji with UTF-8 format

There, that is much better and will be more sustainable in the long term as well. The overall code for this in Google Colab will look like this:

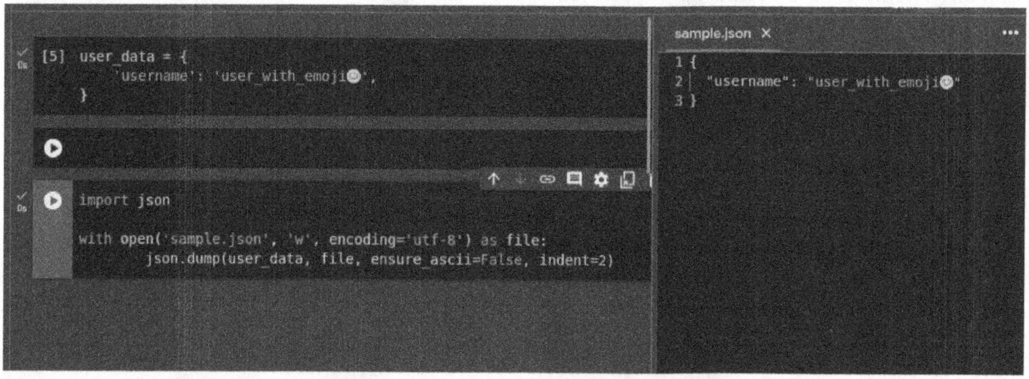

Figure 11.7 – Colab notebook for UTF-8-based storage of emoji

Those were a few simple examples to get you started on optimizing your work with big data. We have talked quite a bit about data and a bit about machine learning. But let's round all of this out with the hottest topic of all: ChatGPT. We will now talk about how the DevOps behind ChatGPT works and how similar open source systems are widely available currently.

The Ops behind ChatGPT

ChatGPT – in the time that I have been writing this book – has gone from being a hot topic to just being a fact of life, sometimes almost second nature as a tool for information. The way it handles data and the very nature of it have been topics that have brought on a lot of controversy. But one of the things that I get asked very often by my friends who aren't in the industry is, how does it work? They see that it delivers information nearly seamlessly on whatever the whim of the user is and then retains that information historically in that chat for future questions. It also does so very quickly. So, one does wonder how it all works.

Let's start with what ChatGPT is: it is a **large language model** (**LLM**), which is a very large neural network that verges on general language understanding (i.e., the ability to understand questions or queries and deliver back responses that would be appropriate to the solution). While ChatGPT is the biggest deal at the moment, the technology itself has been around for a few years, mostly used in more domain-specific chatbots. However, the newest LLMs have been made so that they can talk about pretty much anything, with slight knowledge specializations in certain fields. Even then, the concept behind ChatGPT is pretty simple: the more data you feed into it that it can contain, the better it becomes.

The current free commercial model GPT-3.5 is made up of about 175 billion parameters spread over 96 neural network layers. How it did so was by inputting over 500 billion words as tokens (numbers) and using its neural network to find associations between these tokens in a way that simulates human language. The set used as a reference for these tokens is just the internet. That's it, it takes all the text and data from the internet and uses that to recreate human interaction and creativity. Now, most of you have probably seen what GPT-3/3.5 can do, and GPT-4 ramps that concept up even further, using a total of 1.7 trillion data points. As we can see in the following figure, it is a case of adding some parameters to a neural network until it creates a coherent output:

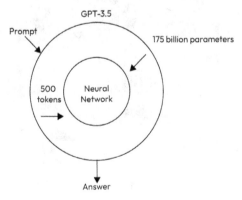

Figure 11.8 – The workflow behind ChatGPT

As seen in the diagram, you put the prompt in and get an answer generated by the trained neural network. It's that simple. Now, you may be wondering, what happens in between? The answer to that is fascinating, but can be boiled down to a concise statement: we don't know.

Truly, neural networks are a mystery because they are built and modeled around our own neurons, so they aren't trained by humans; they train themselves for the best possible success, similar to the way a human would find their best method of study for themselves when trying to pass a test. So, we don't really know what is at the core of these neural networks; we just know we can train them to become good at having a conversation.

You can train a similar one at home, too. Some companies have developed more compressed versions of LLMs that can be placed on smaller servers, such as Meta's **LLaMA**. But even besides that, you can find a never-ending amount of generative AI models on any cloud provider of your preference and on open source sites such as Hugging Face, which you can plug and play to try and understand better.

Summary

The journey of a DataOps or MLOps engineer is just a DevOps engineer who has gotten some understanding of data and machine learning concepts. That's pretty much it. But, as we saw in this chapter, the usage of those concepts is a pretty useful thing.

First, we talked about the differences and similarities between DevOps and these associated fields and how they are connected with each other. Using that, we managed to produce a couple of practical use cases that can come in handy when using Python with DataOps and MLOps.

Next, we talked about handling the proverbial big data. We talked about the aspects that make the data so big and how to tackle each of these aspects individually using a use case for each.

Finally, we talked about ChatGPT and how it works in delivering all the things that it delivers to users around the world. We discussed the simplicity of its complexity and its mystery, as well as the new age of open source LLMs that has accelerated the development of generative AI.

In the next chapter, we will get into perhaps the most powerful tool in the DevOps arsenal, **Infrastructure as Code (IaC)**, and how Python is used in this realm.

12

How Python Integrates with IaC Concepts

Never measure the height of a mountain until you have reached the top. Then you will see how low it was.

– Dag Hammarskjöld

So, as we approach this penultimate chapter, we get to the topic of **Infrastructure as Code (IaC)**. It is quite the topic, indeed, one that has taken the IT world by storm. It is a response to the fact that there are now more resources available for applications and workloads than there ever were before and the only thing left to do is arrange them in the most optimal way. Sure, you might find a way to do this once manually and it might work. But having to do it over and over again with a guarantee that you won't make mistakes? That's foolish talk and a waste of manpower.

So, based on these observations, the concept of IaC emerged. It posited that if resource creation, provisioning, and updating were standardized in the form of code with constants and variables arranged in an organized way, you could standardize the replication of resources, making things such as backups, failovers, re-deployments and a whole lot of other operations activities easier.

Of course, IaC has its detractors, because all good technology does. They believe that it is too fast, too powerful, capable of running up your cloud bill and putting up resources that become too hard to untangle and are not as easily customizable.

It's an interesting thought, but when I look at IaC, I am reminded of the initial passage in Adam Smith's *Wealth of Nations* where he talks about how the division of labor increases production more than any other factor. IaC concepts do the same, where the labor (resources) is separated from the schematics that build them, allowing them to be produced over and over again.

Python as a language has been very friendly towards IaC, perhaps the second-most behind Go. There are a lot of native IaC libraries and stacks in Python (which we will cover), in addition to modules and APIs to interact with IaC tools not written in Python. The flexibility of Python and the desire for loose, yet strict replication that comes with IaC allowed Python to become such a huge part of the growing IaC trend.

This chapter will help you with a concept in IaC that is considered unique to DevOps, one that was created to fuel the constant need for automation and standardization in a DevOps workload. It will help you understand why DevOps and coding need to be so closely related to each other. That is why, in this chapter, you will learn the following:

- The basics of **SaltStack** and how it is built in Python along with how to evaluate SaltStack modules at the code and command-line levels

- The basics of **Ansible** and how to create your own automated Ansible module

- How you can use Python to interact with other IaC tools, such as Terraform, to add automation on top of already built automation

Technical requirements

In order to pursue this chapter to its logical conclusion, you will need to fulfill a few technical requirements:

- Installation of Python with the **Salt library** and Ansible

- Installation of NPM and NodeJS with `cdktf`

- Installation of Terraform CLI

- An AWS and a GCP account

- A GitHub account to retrieve the repository for this book (`https://github.com/PacktPublishing/Hands-On-Python-for-DevOps`)

- A significant amount of patience and understanding

Automation and customization with Python's Salt library

We talk about all of these fancy architectures and frameworks that we want to make; we talk about all of these different tools that we want to use, all of these workflows, and they are fun. They are very exciting, but the thing that a lot of DevOps still boils down to is server management; the Ops side of DevOps. It is still important and relevant in today's world and will be for as long as people use it, which is likely forever.

Server management in the modern day requires the creation of modern, custom environments based on the requirements of the application being hosted. It also requires a lot of automation features to be maintained and to stay in an optimized state based on present circumstances.

The radio was never replaced by the television, and television in turn probably won't be replaced by streaming completely. Everything changes, evolves, or reduces down, but the thing itself and the skills needed to use it will be relevant in one way or another. This is why the tools for server management will always be there and they will evolve.

That's what the Salt library (used interchangeably with SaltStack) is used for. In essence, it consists of a central server that can be used to send commands to all servers connected to it. The requirements are that the minion (server to be managed) is configured to receive commands from the master (server that does the managing). It's a pretty simple concept, executed using only the finest Python code.

So, let's get into it. We will start with the installation of a Salt server and a minion, and then, we will see how we can customize the Python code that comprises Salt if needed.

The architecture of the Salt library consists of, as we said, a master and several minions. So, let's start by creating servers that mirror this configuration:

1. We will create one master server and a minion in GCP, and one minion in AWS to show cross-cloud functionality. For this exercise, we are using Ubuntu as our primary **operating system (OS)**, but other OSs will work just as well. We will make a minion and a master Salt instance in GCP:

Figure 12.1 – Salt instances in GCP

2. We will also add a minion instance in AWS:

Figure 12.2 – Salt instance in AWS

3. Now, we can SSH into the `salt-master` instance and install the Salt master library:

```
sudo apt install salt-master
```

After this, you can run `salt-master --version` to run a check on the installation and get the version, similar to the following:

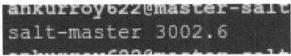

Figure 12.3 – Salt master version

4. Next, install the Salt minion library in both of the minion instances using the following command:

```
sudo apt install salt-minion
```

Then, run `salt-minion --version` in order to verify installation and get the version, similar to the following:

```
ubuntu@ip-172-31-41-27:~$ salt-minion --version
salt-minion 3004.1
```

Figure 12.4 – Salt minion version

5. Next, go back to the Salt master and run the following command:

```
sudo nano /etc/salt/master
```

6. After we have done so, we will insert the following lines at the bottom to account for interfacing between the master and the minions:

```
interface: 0.0.0.0
publish_port: 4505
ret_port: 4506
auto_accept: True
```

7. Next, we will run `sudo systemctl start salt-master` to initialize the Salt master system module, then run the `sudo systemctl status salt-master` command to get the status of the Salt master. When we run the command, we get something like the following:

```
● salt-master.service - The Salt Master Server
     Loaded: loaded (/lib/systemd/system/salt-master.service; enabled; vendor preset: enabled)
     Active: active (running) since Tue 2024-01-02 22:05:37 UTC; 51min ago
       Docs: man:salt-master(1)
             file:///usr/share/doc/salt/html/contents.html
             https://docs.saltstack.com/en/latest/contents.html
   Main PID: 1580 (salt-master)
      Tasks: 32 (limit: 4691)
```

Figure 12.5 – Running Salt master server

That is a running Salt master; now, we need to configure our minions.

The steps to configuring the minions are similar to those for the master, but with a few differences, as we will explore here:

1. On each minion, run `sudo nano /etc/salt/minion`, and in the nano file, enter the following:

    ```
    master: <salt_master_ip>
    ```

    Replace `salt_master_ip` with the IP of your Salt master server.

2. Then, run `sudo systemctl start salt-minion`, which will initialize the minion. Then, run `sudo systemctl status salt-minion` to check whether the minion is running:

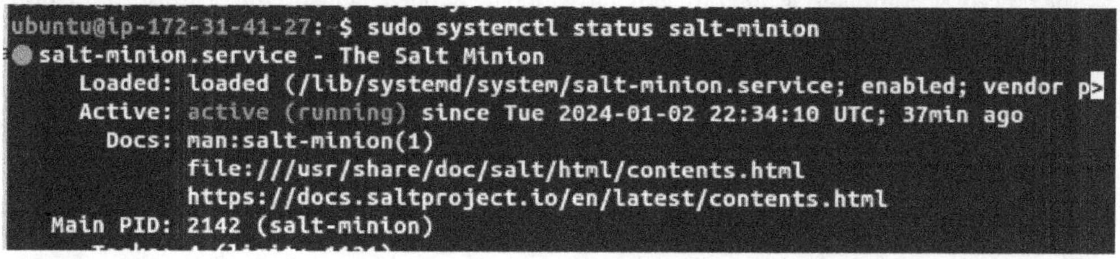

```
ubuntu@ip-172-31-41-27: $ sudo systemctl status salt-minion
salt-minion.service - The Salt Minion
   Loaded: loaded (/lib/systemd/system/salt-minion.service; enabled; vendor p>
   Active: active (running) since Tue 2024-01-02 22:34:10 UTC; 37min ago
     Docs: man:salt-minion(1)
           file:///usr/share/doc/salt/html/contents.html
           https://docs.saltproject.io/en/latest/contents.html
 Main PID: 2142 (salt-minion)
```

Figure 12.6 – Running Salt minion

3. Now, on the Salt master, you can run a little example command as follows:

    ```
    sudo salt '*' test.ping
    ```

That's the basics of it. Now, let's move to the part where we look at the Python code a little closer.

Let's break down a particular Salt module so that we can learn the intricacies behind it:

1. Each Salt module is a Python function that can be called. Let's take one module as an example from the documentation, in this case, the one for network connections:

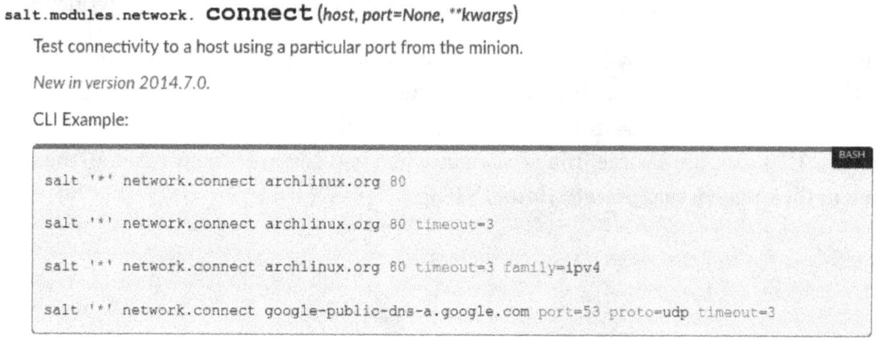

`salt.modules.network.` **connect** *(host, port=None, **kwargs)*

Test connectivity to a host using a particular port from the minion.

New in version 2014.7.0.

CLI Example:

```
salt '*' network.connect archlinux.org 80

salt '*' network.connect archlinux.org 80 timeout=3

salt '*' network.connect archlinux.org 80 timeout=3 family=ipv4

salt '*' network.connect google-public-dns-a.google.com port=53 proto=udp timeout=3
```

Figure 12.7 – Salt module from the documentation

This is great documentation! It shows you the function and the CLI version for it.

2. Let's look at the function:

```
connect(host, port=None, **kwargs)
```

The `connect` function takes a hostname compulsorily and it takes a port number optionally. It also includes `**kwargs`, which is just a large number of arguments such as `proto` and `timeout` that the function may have. The following command connects to a DNS instance:

```
salt '*' network.connect google-public-dns-a.google.com port=53
proto=udp timeout=3
```

The preceding command is for connecting to a Google public DNS with the `connect` function. An equivalent in code would be as follows:

```
connect("google-public-dns-a.google.com", port = 53, proto =
"udp", timeout = 3)
```

These two commands are equivalent, but you can see the pragmatism in running them from the command line, as these commands are far more comfortable in that way than as functions.

That stands true for a lot of command-line tools and is the reason that a lot of them exist in the first place.

Next, we will look at Ansible, which has a similar idea to execute but takes a slightly different approach while still using Python.

How Ansible works and the Python code behind it

A lot of this section will be more of the same that you saw in the previous section, similar tools, similar implementations, and whatnot. But, like SaltStack, this too is an important and very common tool in the IaC realm, which is why it deserves the coverage that we are giving it. Ansible is powerful, its learning curve is probably not as steep as that of SaltStack, and it is easier on users who like more cleanly pre-packaged code that they don't have to modify too much. Oh, and it's also written in Python.

Ansible is run and maintained by IBM under its Red Hat label (I like that tech companies have their own *DC Vertigo*-esque labels for their more risque stuff now; it really makes the things I say about it being an art even more true). It is meant to maintain and affect servers using SSH key pairs to access those servers. That simplifies some things, such as when you control a server and all the associated servers are in the same **virtual private cloud** (**VPC**).

Ansible is a bit more flexible in terms of the OSs that you can control with it, but for this exercise, we will use old, reliable Ubuntu. With all that exposition out of the way, let's get into the finicky details of Ansible and give you a little sample of how it works.

We will be reusing the same instances used during the Salt exercise for this, so let's start with the master instance:

1. Let's start by using `pip` to install Ansible on the system:

    ```
    pip install ansible ansible-inventory
    ```

    Sometimes you may need to install `pip` as well, though that is not a frequent occurrence. Let's run this command and install Ansible:

    ```
    Successfully built ansible-inventory
    Installing collected packages: resolvelib, async-timeout, redis, ansible-core, a
    nsible-inventory, ansible
    Successfully installed ansible-9.1.0 ansible-core-2.16.2 ansible-inventory-0.6.4
    ```

    Figure 12.8 – Successful Ansible installation

2. Once you have done this, make a directory to use as the common Ansible configuration directory and go into it:

    ```
    mkdir ansible_project
    cd ansible_project
    ```

3. The next thing to do is to create an `inventory.ini` file, which will serve the same function as the master IP in SaltStack but in reverse, with the IPs of the servers being controlled and placed in the controlling server.

4. Run `sudo nano inventory.ini`, which will create the inventory file, and place a list of IP addresses that you want to run in there:

    ```
    [myhosts]
    <IP_1>
    <IP_2>
    ```

5. Now, you can run the `ansible-inventory -i inventory.ini --list` command and this will give you the following list of hosts:

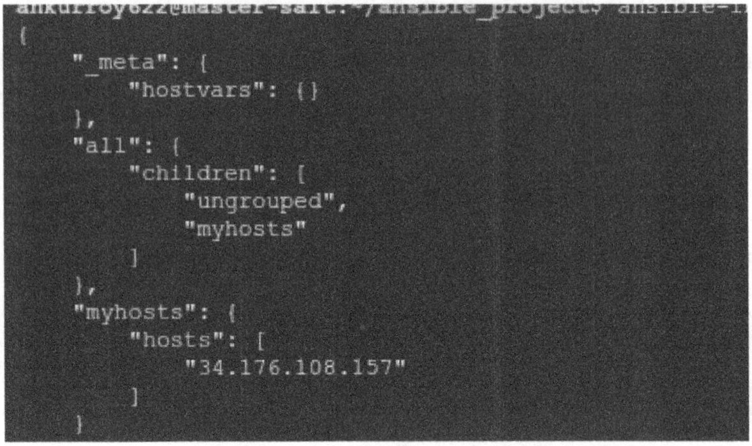

Figure 12.9 - Ansible inventory

6. Next, you can ping these hosts to test your connection with the following command:

```
ansible myhosts -m ping -i inventory.ini
```

7. Now, you can run playbooks and runbooks through a centralized command server and you can even sort the hosts into fleets just by changing the inventory list.

Those are the basics of Ansible; now, let's look a little deeper and find the Python behind the CLI as we did with SaltStack. We will do so by creating a custom module to use with Ansible. We'll keep it local this time, but this is basically how you run custom operations with Ansible all the time.

Now, let's create a new Ansible module, custom-made by us:

1. In the environment where you have installed Ansible, create a `hello_ansible.py` file and add the following code to it:

```python
from ansible.module_utils.basic import AnsibleModule
def join_strings(string_1, string_2):
    return string_1+string_2
def main():
    module_args = dict(
        string_1=dict(type='str', required=True),
        string_2=dict(type='str', required=True),
    )
    result = dict(changed=False, message="" )
    module = AnsibleModule(
        argument_spec=module_args,
```

```
            supports_check_mode=True
        )
        string_1 = module.params['string_1']
        string_2 = module.params['string_2']
        result["message"] = string_1 + " " + string_2
        module.exit_json(**result)

if __name__ == '__main__':
    main()
```

That gives us the Python code that will be executed and now we need to change the Python code's permissions into something executable. We do this by using the following command:

```
chmod +x hello_ansible.py
```

2. Next, we need to make a playbook to run the function locally, and for that, we can create a playbook called `hello.yml` and add some code to it:

```
---
- hosts: localhost
  gather_facts: false
  tasks:
    - name: Hello World
      add_numbers:
        string_1: Hello
        string_2: Ansible
      register: result

    - debug:
        var: result
```

3. Now, execute the YAML file:

```
ansible-playbook -M . hello.yml
```

This will give you a result as a string, shown as follows:

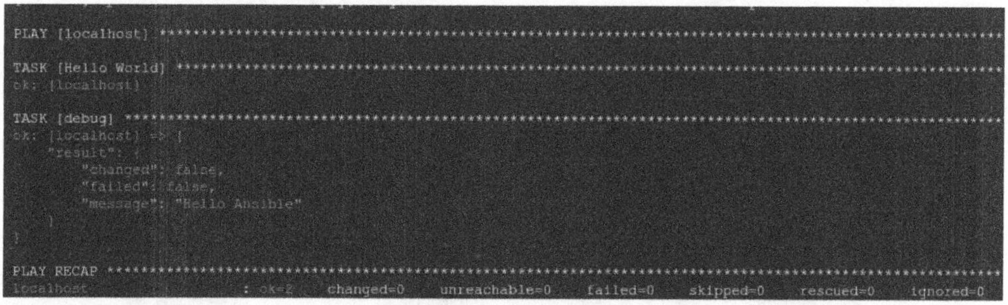

Figure 12.10 – Result of our Ansible module

That is how you create a customized Ansible module. This module will give you the sum of two strings that you put into it, perhaps the most basic operation that you can do with a module. But everything else is the same, even for more complex operations. Just replace join_strings in the code with the function of your choice and add the variables needed to execute that function and return the resulting value. Maybe, for example, it could be a function to restart a server or run a particular CLI command; it can be practically anything that you can do on a command line in the OS that you are using.

Now, even this is a little bit underpowered in terms of the resources that you can use and the way that you can use them. It is useful for more conventional systems, but for systems that require unconventional architectures, something like Terraform is better suited. We will now discuss how we can use Terraform with Python to automate IaC even further.

Automate the automation of IaC with Python

IaC has grown in popularity and in ways that people have never imagined. The most popular IaC framework currently is arguably Terraform. Terraform doesn't just work on servers and more solid resources of the like, it works on APIs and looser infrastructure as well. Basically, anything that you can use in any major cloud, there is a Terraform API to use it. Terraform is the ultimate automation tool in many ways, and it can be further automated with the help of Python.

Terraform is, of course, written in Go, which is great because Go is a very good complement to Python. One is good where the other lacks and vice versa. While Go is good for singular implementations, Python is great at multiplying the effectiveness of that implementation. Basically, Go is the bullet and Python is the gun, and that is an effective combination. We will use this combination to great effect in this section.

HashiCorp, the creator of Terraform, has created APIs that allow Python to interact with Terraform. These APIs are packaged in the cdktf library published by HashiCorp in a number of languages. Let's take a look at the steps we need to perform to install and run the cdktf library:

1. You need to first have NPM, NodeJS, and the Terraform CLI installed to install cdktf-cli:

   ```
   npm install -g cdktf-cli
   ```

2. Next, you can use the cdktf to create a Python environment:

   ```
   cdktf init --template=python
   ```

3. This will create a new Python template, which can be used then to run a Terraform template. In the template, you can find the main.py file in the stacks folder. In the folder, you can add this script:

   ```
   from constructs import Construct
   from cdktf import App, TerraformStack
   from imports.aws import AwsProvider, S3Bucket
   ```

```
class MyStack(TerraformStack):
    def __init__(self, scope: Construct, ns: str):
        super().__init__(scope, ns)
        AwsProvider(self, 'Aws', region='us-east-1')
        S3Bucket(
            self,
            '<Terraform_Function_Name>',
            bucket=<'Bucket_Name_Here>',
            acl='private'
        )
app = App()
MyStack(app, "python-cdktf")
app.synth()
```

4. This code is simple enough to understand; it works exactly like an IaC module would, creating an S3 bucket with the name given at the time of your execution of the program. To execute the program, run the following command:

    cdktf deploy

5. If you want to revert the program and simply delete the resource that you created, you can just run the following command:

    cdktf destroy

That is basically all you need to do. The AWS, Google Cloud, and Azure modules for Terraform are usually included with the installation, as are the equivalent Python libraries when they are installed using cdktf. You can find the documentation for all of these libraries and what they do on HashiCorp's GitHub and on its website. HashiCorp is very clear about the things that its products can do, even if it is sometimes difficult to collate all of that information in one place. So, using these references, you can practically create any resource you want; it is all up to your imagination.

Summary

So, that is the chapter, one that was a little more serious than the ones you might have been used to, but this is serious business. IaC is a concept to be taken seriously; it is very powerful and can be the solution to a lot of problems that require the application of DevOps principles.

We initially looked at a very basic application of IaC using Python in SaltStack. It was quite rudimentary but very effective for simple projects. We closed it out by diving into the guts of SaltStack and understanding the logic behind its Python modules.

After that, we looked at the slightly more flexible Ansible and discovered all of the conveniences that it provides as well as the customization possibilities.

Lastly, we looked at Terraform and `cdktf`, which is used with Python Terraform and resource modules in order to perform Terraform's resource creation.

All of this has hopefully helped you gain a new perspective on IaC and allowed you to understand its importance in DevOps and its integration with Python.

In conclusion, IaC is powerful, vast, and useful to learn. In the next chapter, we will take all that you have learned here and in the previous chapters, and raise it all to a higher level.

13

The Tools to Take Your DevOps to the Next Level

I do nothing but go about persuading you all, old and young alike, not to take thought for your persons or your properties, but and chiefly to care about the greatest improvement of the soul.

– Socrates

Alright, here we are, the final chapter, the final stop on our journey together in this book. It has been fun; I hope you've learned a few things – I certainly have experienced a lot of joy in teaching you and trying to help you in your journey. This whole book has been a journey for me as well. We will now conclude with a few tools that will help you further your journey into DevOps and Python on your own.

Consider this chapter to be an epilogue: a quick perusal of everything that has happened over the course of this book and a recap of all your learnings put into a functional context. In *The Lord of the Rings*, when the war is over, we see all of the characters have their individual endings of how their lives continued. That is my aim with this chapter, to leave you with something that rouses your curiosity and encourages you to walk even further down this path of DevOps and learn for yourselves what you can achieve.

On a personal note, I can say that over the course of writing this book, I have changed in many ways as well. The concepts of collaboration that I have preached throughout this book have come to help me greatly in collaborating with all of the wonderful people who have made this book possible. It has helped me level up in a way, and has pushed the boundaries of my ability and made me understand the responsibility of being an author.

The journeys that we undertake change us, mostly for the better. They make us confront who we are and what we want to do. The journey that I undertook writing this book has made me appreciative of the knowledge I had beforehand and the knowledge that I gained during the research of this book. It has made me a professional writer, and while this book won't be as big a part of your life as it was mine, I hope it has helped facilitate your journey as well.

So, for the final time, in this chapter, you will learn about the following:

- Advanced automation tools that will allow you to make even more complex automation into a reality
- Advanced monitoring tools to combine your monitoring and data analysis workloads and use both skills
- Advanced event response strategies for when those events and alerts really get out of hand

Technical requirements

To follow along with this chapter, you will require the following:

- A Grafana account at `grafana.com`
- An AWS account with the ability to use AWS Step Functions and Compute Engine
- A GitHub account to use the code in this book's repository (`https://github.com/PacktPublishing/Hands-On-Python-for-DevOps`)
- A Google Cloud Platform project with Google Kubernetes API enabled
- A sense of achievement that you have reached this far in your learning process

Advanced automation tools

Throughout this book, I have emphasized the value of automation and how important it is to the DevOps realm and the increase of your productivity in general. It is very hard to go overboard with automation as long as you're careful with it and understand your use case. We have expanded our toolbelts throughout this book to allow us to automate tasks in a number of scenarios. We even figured out how to automate those automations. But now, let's look into a tool that may take this process a step further. It also happens to be a personal favorite of mine.

AWS Step Functions is something that I am always excited to talk about and use. Whenever I look for the gold standard of automation workflow tools, it is this that I think of. Any other automation tool that I have seen that works well has had very similar functionality and usability to Step Functions. There are, of course, equivalent services in the other major clouds that can be used as a replacement and that work well in those environments, but the UX on Step Functions is the one that I prefer and is the one that will be the easiest to explain in this workflow.

Let's go into a few steps (and steps inside of steps) in Step Functions:

1. Log in to your AWS account, and on the console, search for `Step Functions`.
2. Go to the **Step Functions** page, and at the top right, click on **Create state machine**.

Figure 13.1 – Creating a state machine

The Step Functions workflow consists of actions, which are the invocation of services, completely based on the parameters that their APIs take, and flows, which direct the flow of the data.

The example function that we will demonstrate consists entirely of flows since using actions simply requires calling APIs, and you can apply them wherever you see fit. Here is a diagram of this flow:

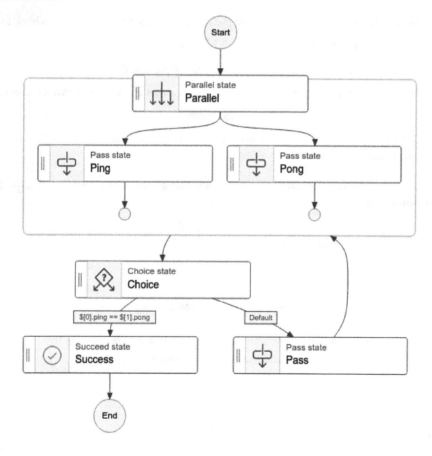

Figure 13.2 – State machine diagram

This was exported directly from the Step Functions console, which you can see here:

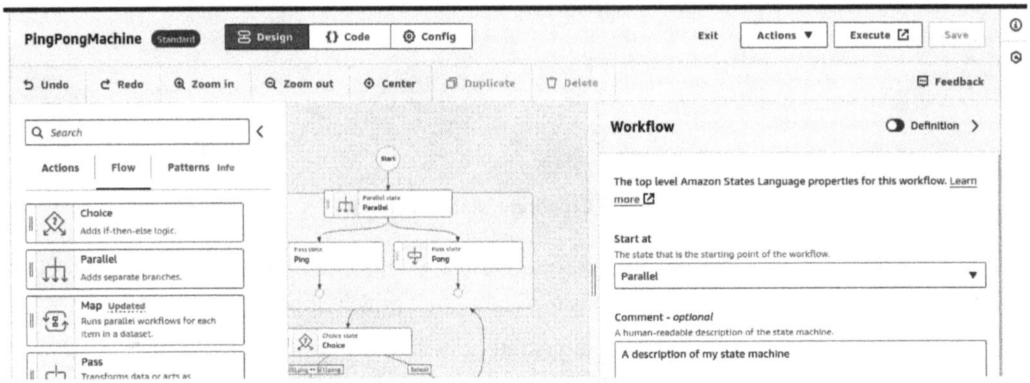

Figure 13.3 – State machine console

It has also been exported in code format and placed in the GitHub repository of this book for use. We can break down the diagram in *Figure 13.2* like this:

I.   The parallel state runs two different functions, **Ping** and **Pong**.

II.   Both of them produce random numbers between a start and end value that the user inputs.

III.   Once this is done, both numbers are compared to see which one is greater than the other.

IV.   If **Ping** is greater than **Pong**, the state machine stops its execution; otherwise, it executes the parallel state instead.

3.   Once you have saved your state machine, you can access it and run it using the **Start execution** button.

Step Functions > State machines > State machine: PingPongMachine

PingPongMachine   Edit   Actions ▼   Start execution

Figure 13.4 – Starting an execution on a state machine

4.   You will be asked what you would want to input in this state machine. In this case, we will choose the starting number as 5 and the ending number as 100.

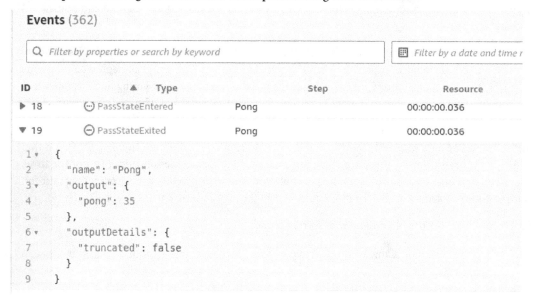

```
1 ▾ {
2        "start":5,
3        "end":100
4    }
```

Figure 13.5 – Parameters given to start the state machine

5. The machine will go until **Ping** and **Pong** give us equal values, which takes about two seconds for numbers as small as this.

6. Step Functions logs all of the states that it passes, along with the results:

Events (362)

| | Q Filter by properties or search by keyword | | 🗓 Filter by a date and time r |

ID	▲ Type	Step	Resource
▶ 18	⊙ PassStateEntered	Pong	00:00:00.036
▼ 19	⊖ PassStateExited	Pong	00:00:00.036

```
1 ▾ {
2        "name": "Pong",
3 ▾      "output": {
4           "pong": 35
5        },
6 ▾      "outputDetails": {
7           "truncated": false
8        }
9    }
```

Figure 13.6 – Events that occurred during the state machine

This particular application seems rather mundane, but it is a great proof of concept for how Step Functions can be used to make workflows. An example of a real-world application for this could be a simple one that we have used before: deleting all the objects in an S3 bucket. There is no clear way in the user interface of AWS to delete all your objects at once; you need to do it one by one. But with Step Functions (which is integrated with every AWS service), you can list out and delete all the objects in an S3 bucket in parallel if you want to. Now, we will pivot to the monitoring of such applications to learn some insights into how to make them even better.

Advanced monitoring tools

The purpose behind monitoring has always been to make sure that the things you said were working are still working. And it is often the case that they won't be. It could be your fault or not; the concept of fault gets in the way of solving the problem. The proper monitoring of your workloads provides the path to more easily solving your problems.

The simplest workloads can be monitored and the reactions to the information received can be automated so that you don't even have to be involved most of the time when it comes to dealing with something going wrong. In more complex workloads, it is still important to keep up monitoring for faster reaction times to any situation, as well as to get more information on the situation in real time.

Often, your solution, as it gets more complex, starts using more tools. More tools and services means the requirement for more monitoring and also more complex monitoring. If your monitoring comes from multiple places at the same time, it can become quite a hassle to deal with. So, a good solution in this case would be to centralize the monitoring in a central location that can hold and manage all of that data.

This is where **Grafana** comes in, and it is the tool I want to talk about because it provides not only a ridiculously wide range of monitoring options but also an incredible range of deployment options with which you can make your Grafana instance managed or customized, meaning that it is a solution for both kinds of people: those who prefer self-made solutions and those who prefer ready-made.

When I first started looking into Grafana, I was writing a blog on how to monitor multiple compute instances over several different clouds using the monitoring services of one cloud, and I found that while that is pretty simple, there are still a few awkward hitches to the solution. Most of the time, choosing one cloud over the other resulted in complications arising in other services on the platform. A lot of these problems were solved by Grafana and all the love and work that has gone into making it.

So, let's dive into the use of Grafana with its free account tier:

1. Firstly, create a Grafana account. It is completely free and has a lot of SSO options, which I appreciate.

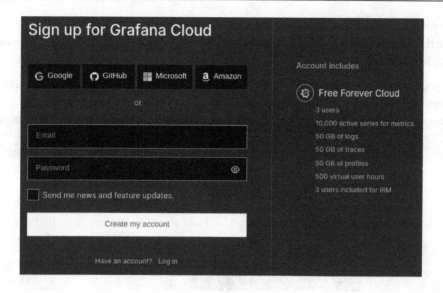

Figure 13.7 – Grafana signup

2. It will then ask you for your own personal monitoring subdomain URL and the region for deploying your instance. Once you set those, you are good to go.

3. Alternatively, you can download and install Grafana on a custom server from here: `https://grafana.com/grafana/download?edition=oss`. It has installation instructions for practically every OS that you can think of.

4. Let's take a look at our dashboard:

Figure 13.8 – Grafana dashboard

As you can see, Grafana offers us a lot of monitoring options, integrations, and data sources. For this exercise, we will use a data source that is very ubiquitous that just about anyone can access: Google Sheets.

5. In your console's search tab, search for Google Sheets. You will then have to install the plugin. It is the blue button at the far right:

Figure 13.9 – Google Sheets connector

6. Then, wait a minute for the plugin to install, and add a new data source from that same page.

Figure 13.10 – Google Sheets connector activated

7. Grafana will then ask you to create authentication credentials for your Google Sheets instance that you want to access, and it will even give you the proper instructions to do so.

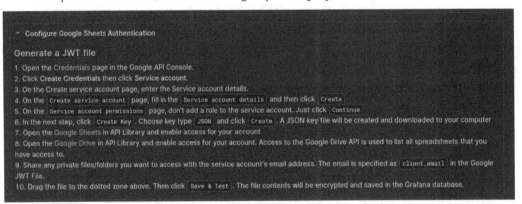

Figure 13.11 – Instructions provided by Grafana on its dashboard

In this case, security-wise, the JWT token option is probably the best. You do not want to keep stray API keys lying around; therefore, please do the following:

I.   Follow the steps given to create a service account and give that service account's email address access to your sample Google Sheet.

II. Once you have uploaded your JWT key, you will have access to anything that the service account we used has access to. I used a Google Sheet that contained some sample web traffic data, but you can use any sheet that you want for this operation.

The cache time for this dashboard has been set to zero seconds, meaning that it will refresh as the information on the Google Sheet changes.

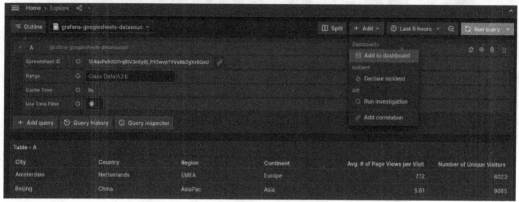

Figure 13.12 – Sample exploration with the option to add to a dashboard

You can then add this exploration to a new monitoring dashboard. As seen in *Figure 13.12*, you can select the **Add** button and then the **Add to dashboard** option.

Figure 13.13 – Creating a new dashboard with a panel

8. This will create a new dashboard with your data table. We can now add some visualizations for our data on top of it. In the new dashboard, click on **Add** and then **Visualization**. You'll get a panel similar to the one for the Google Sheets table where you can add a chart like this:

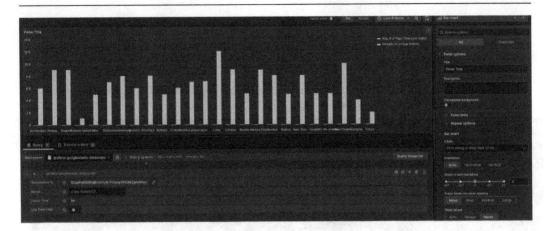

Figure 13.14 – Bar graph produced by visualization

You can see we have a highly customizable chart containing all of the information in a visualized form.

Once you have made your visualization, go back to your newly created dashboard. Your final visualization will look something like this:

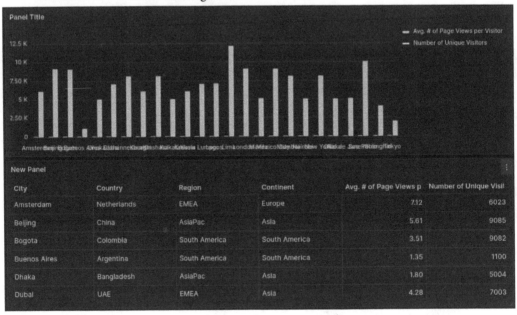

Figure 13.15 – Final Grafana dashboard

Again, this changes according to changes in data.

So far, we have seen events and automations that deal with events. But what happens when an event occurs that you can't just reset your way out of? What happens when you are on the back foot and are forced to run damage control? Well, we are going to find out in the next section.

Advanced event response strategies

An event response should be simple and organized, and it should bring about the solution to whatever caused the event in the first place. But, once again, no matter how hard we try, it is never that simple. Sometimes you're working with a system you haven't had the chance to work with much. Sometimes the team that you work with is not experienced enough to help out in any meaningful way. These circumstances cannot be helped because of time and personnel constraints, and they are largely out of our control. In such situations, we simply have to make do with what we have.

But there is one scenario that happens very often and causes widespread damage to the point where the response to the event stops being about damage recovery and starts being about what you can recover from the damage already done. This will occur if any sort of incident goes unreported or unmonitored for a long period of time. These situations often occur when there is some sort of data breach, or an unknown/undiscovered error is present in the system.

So, what do you do when you suffer such a scenario? Well, the first thing to do is not to panic. But don't think *don't panic* – that'll make you panic more! Approach the situation logically. I will now give you insight into how I would approach such a situation. It is based on situations that I have faced in the past, as well as everything I have learned about problem-solving from all sorts of places. I think it's a good way to solve a lot of problems, IT or otherwise. So let's get into it.

Step 0: Read

Because: You don't do that enough

Seriously, a lot of errors can be solved just by reading the outputs of those errors or glitches. Trust the thing you see and you will be rewarded; the solutions to your problems lie right in front of you. Well, the first steps to the solutions, anyway. But if you want to get there, you need to read and understand the process of getting there. You cannot get to step 1 without knowing all of the details in front of you.

Step 1: If it is a single problem, google it

Because: You are not alone.

This is serious advice. 90% of any sort of error that you encounter can be solved by Googling the error. This is because someone else has probably encountered your problem before. They have probably had the correct solution given to them before too. Chances are really high that you will find the solution to your problem on a *Stack Overflow* forum, a GitHub repository comment, an obscure YouTube video, or somewhere like that. You might be thinking to yourself: "It's not that easy – no way can I solve my biggest problems just by googling them." Stop thinking that right now! I once saw someone spend a full two hours trying a migration bridge, which we managed in about five minutes after looking at a

YouTube tutorial. It happens – stop wasting your time and look for quick, informed results. They'll handle the minor problems, and believe me, most problems are minor.

Step 2: If it is several problems, google it several times (or, now, ChatGPT it)

Because: One big problem is several small problems combined into one

It's true: any problem can be broken down into its smallest components and solved at that level. It is basic logic; if you have a big problem, turn it into smaller problems and google those. If it is a really big problem or breaking down the problem will be mundane and take a lot of your time, you can use ChatGPT for that now; it is fairly good at that. Digesting a large amount of useless text into smaller, useful versions is probably what ChatGPT is best at. Use it. Use these great tools that you have at your disposal.

Step 3: Follow the methods of induction and deduction

Because: It will solve any everyday problem you have

Solutions and solving problems are very different from having ideas. Ideas are like lightning bolts from God; they are ghosts in our system, appearing out of the oddest of places. Grabbing an idea and bringing it to fruition is an ethereal experience, like having a religious revelation. Solutions are not that. They are simple, fundamental, and – if you know how to solve a problem – much easier to approach. The logic can be summarized in two words: induction and deduction.

Every major problem that I have ever solved where I had access to a sample environment, I have solved with this logic. It's something I found in *Zen and the Art of Motorcycle Maintenance*, where the narrator solves the most mundane problems through these two methods and connects these concepts to those of quantum physics and Zen Buddhism. These are not complex concepts, but all problem-solving can be defined within their parameters.

Induction is recreating the elements that cause the problem in a system to know exactly where the problem has occurred. This is useful in incident management when an incident needs to be recreated in a sample application and then breaking down those steps to find out where it all went wrong.

Deduction is starting at the end and going back to the beginning. This is used when the logic of the error is not recreatable or an incident has occurred already with no idea of how it occurred. In this case, you work back from the end result and figure out what could possibly have caused these results.

So, summarizing these results in a diagram, you can look at them like this:

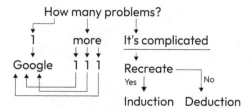

Figure 13.16 – The steps to solving any IT problem you want

And that is how you solve all of your problems. Try it out on a few of them and see how far you get. If you want to know about the formation of ideas, well, they are quite random, but they can be specified and turned into action points based on methods similar to these. So, now you have learned everything. Use your knowledge wisely.

Summary

Alright, this is the end, not just of the chapter but of the book. The end of your journey as a reader of this book and of mine as a first-time author. It has been quite the journey. Talking about this chapter in general, it was a lot more abstract and a lot less code-focused than a lot of the other chapters, but that is because I've come to understand one thing when it comes to all of these systems: everything is code. Everything you touch will have been coded in some way; it is just up to you to understand and manipulate the logic behind it.

In the section regarding Step Functions, you learned about a very useful automation tool, but you also learned that it is a way to use coding logic visually while integrating that way into a lot of powerful tools and services.

In the section on advanced monitoring, we learned about a powerful monitoring and visualization tool in Grafana and the importance of centralized monitoring in preserving your sanity by not having to look through data from multiple locations and then parsing through them, and instead having one location that will work for all your workloads.

Finally, you learned about how I approach problem-solving, an effective method if I do say so myself. I hope you get the chance to use it on your own workloads. This is a sort of meta code, an algorithm that is not beholden to any platform or technology but will work effectively on all of them.

And so, I must bid you adieu. We have come to the end, but look at it only as the end of the beginning, because what happens after is the most important part. This is what will define the person you are and the things that you will do. Now comes the part where you apply all of this knowledge in your own daily dealings. *Remember: the power is with you; it is time to use it.*

Index

Symbols

`packtpub.com`

Subscribe to our online digital library for full access to over 7,000 books and videos, as well as industry leading tools to help you plan your personal development and advance your career. For more information, please visit our website.

Why subscribe?

- Spend less time learning and more time coding with practical eBooks and Videos from over 4,000 industry professionals

- Improve your learning with Skill Plans built especially for you

- Get a free eBook or video every month

- Fully searchable for easy access to vital information

- Copy and paste, print, and bookmark content

Did you know that Packt offers eBook versions of every book published, with PDF and ePub files available? You can upgrade to the eBook version at `packtpub.com` and as a print book customer, you are entitled to a discount on the eBook copy. Get in touch with us at `customercare@packtpub.com` for more details.

At `www.packtpub.com`, you can also read a collection of free technical articles, sign up for a range of free newsletters, and receive exclusive discounts and offers on Packt books and eBooks.

Other Books You May Enjoy

If you enjoyed this book, you may be interested in these other books by Packt:

Go for DevOps

John Doak, David Justice

ISBN: 978-1-80181-889-6

- Understand the basic structure of the Go language to begin your DevOps journey
- Interact with filesystems to read or stream data
- Communicate with remote services via REST and gRPC
- Explore writing tools that can be used in the DevOps environment
- Develop command-line operational software in Go
- Work with popular frameworks to deploy production software
- Create GitHub actions that streamline your CI/CD process
- Write a ChatOps application with Slack to simplify production visibility

Python Essentials for AWS Cloud Developers

Serkan Sakinmaz

ISBN: 978-1-80461-006-0

- Understand the fundamentals of AWS services for Python programming
- Find out how to configure AWS services to build Python applications
- Run and deploy Python applications using Lambda, EC2, and Elastic Beanstalk
- Provision EC2 servers on AWS and run Python applications
- Debug and monitor Python applications using PyCharm and CloudWatch
- Understand database operations on AWS by learning about DynamoDB and RDS
- Explore the API gateway service on AWS using Python to grasp API programming

Packt is searching for authors like you

If you're interested in becoming an author for Packt, please visit `authors.packtpub.com` and apply today. We have worked with thousands of developers and tech professionals, just like you, to help them share their insight with the global tech community. You can make a general application, apply for a specific hot topic that we are recruiting an author for, or submit your own idea.

Share Your Thoughts

Now you've finished *Hands-On Python for DevOps*, we'd love to hear your thoughts! Scan the QR code below to go straight to the Amazon review page for this book and share your feedback or leave a review on the site that you purchased it from.

https://packt.link/r/1835081169

Your review is important to us and the tech community and will help us make sure we're delivering excellent quality content.

Download a free PDF copy of this book

Thanks for purchasing this book!

Do you like to read on the go but are unable to carry your print books everywhere?

Is your eBook purchase not compatible with the device of your choice?

Don't worry, now with every Packt book you get a DRM-free PDF version of that book at no cost.

Read anywhere, any place, on any device. Search, copy, and paste code from your favorite technical books directly into your application.

The perks don't stop there, you can get exclusive access to discounts, newsletters, and great free content in your inbox daily

Follow these simple steps to get the benefits:

1. Scan the QR code or visit the link below

https://packt.link/free-ebook/9781835081167

2. Submit your proof of purchase
3. That's it! We'll send your free PDF and other benefits to your email directly

www.ingramcontent.com/pod-product-compliance
Lightning Source LLC
Chambersburg PA
CBHW080525060326

40690CB00022B/5025